THE PANOPTICON WRITINGS

JEREMY BENTHAM,
with an introduction by Miran Božovič

VERSO
London • New York

This edition first published by Verso 1995
© Verso 1995
Introduction © Miran Božovič 1995

3 5 7 9 10 8 6 4 2

Verso
UK: 6 Meard Street, London W1F 0EG
US: 20 Jay Street, Suite 1010, Brooklyn, NY 11201
www.versobooks.com

Verso is the imprint of New Left Books

ISBN-13: 978-1-84467-666-8

British Library Cataloguing in Publication Data
A catalogue record for this book is available from the British Library

Library of Congress Cataloging-in-Publication Data
A catalog record for this book is available from the Library of Congress

Typeset by Hewer Text UK Ltd, Edinburgh
Printed by in the US by Maple Vail

CONTENTS

INTRODUCTION

'An utterly dark spot'

Miran Božovič

I BENTHAM'S PANOPTICON AND ONTOLOGY OF FICTIONS

Although his main interest was in moral and political philosophy and legislation, it is through the panopticon and the theory of fictions that Jeremy Bentham made his most powerful impact on modern thought. The panopticon was brought to the attention of the wider public in 1975 in Michel Foucault's famed *Surveiller et punir: Naissance de la prison* and Jacques-Alain Miller's brilliant article 'Le Despotisme de l'Utile: la machine panoptique de Jeremy Bentham'; and the theory of fictions was 'rediscovered' in 1932 by C.K. Ogden in a book entitled *Bentham's Theory of Fictions*. It is the panopticon and the theory of fictions that prove Bentham was not only 'a great reformer in philosophy' but, contrary to the opinion of J.S. Mill, also 'a great philosopher'.

The panopticon writings consist of series of *Letters* written from Russia in 1787 'to a friend in England', and two *Postscripts* written in 1790 and 1791 (although printed in 1791, these panopticon writings never found their way into bookshops). The panopticon is nothing more than 'a simple idea in architecture', never realized, describing 'a new mode of obtaining power of mind over mind, in a quantity hitherto without example' – the possessor of this power is 'the inspector' with his invisible omnipresence, 'an utterly dark spot' in the all-transparent, light-flooded universe of the panopticon. The panopticon scheme developed in the *Letters* is endlessly elaborated upon in both *Postscripts* to the extent that the original plan for an all-transparent, panoptic inspection-house becomes to a certain extent opaque, and the idea itself unworkable.

With the exception of the *Fragment on Ontology*, Bentham's writings on fictions, for the most part written in the 1810s, are fragmentary, primarily in the form of digressions from, or footnotes and appendices to, texts on other subjects. Most of these writings were first published posthumously in volume VIII of the Bowring edition under the title *Ontology, Logic, Language*. Not all the writings are consistent with one another or even with themselves. In each text Bentham develops the idea from the beginning, always from a slightly different angle, as if a definite account of fictions were not possible. It is perhaps because in Bentham's eyes reality is unproblematic and its existence unquestionable that things become complicated in the field of the unreal, the non-existent, i.e. in the field of fictions.

In the elaboration of his ontology of fictions, Bentham is less interested in distinguishing fictions from reality, or between fictions themselves, than he is in exploring the effects that fictions have on reality. Although neither of the two main classes of fictions or unreal entities – fictitious entities and imaginary non-entities – exist, both nonetheless have effects on reality: the former *despite the fact that they do not exist*, and the latter *precisely because of the fact that they do not exist*. The main thrust of the *Fragment on Ontology* is that fictitious entities lend reality its logical–discursive consistency. And the main thrust of the panopticon writings is that a certain reality – the panopticon prison – is sustained in existence by something that is utterly unreal, that is, by an imaginary non-entity; it is through its very non-existence that the non-entity sustains the reality in existence – if it were to exist, the reality itself would disintegrate.

II THE SPECTACLE OF PUNISHMENT

As Bentham today is remembered as the founder of utilitarianism, it is perhaps best to start by looking at how the problematic of fictions relates to the moral problematic of crime and its punishment.

In a passage in the *Introduction to the Principles of Morals and Legislation*, which is strongly reminiscent of Leibniz's *Theodicy*, Bentham writes:

[A]ll punishment is mischief: all punishment in itself is evil. Upon the principle of utility, if it ought at all to be admitted, it ought only to be admitted in as far as it promises to exclude some greater evil.[1]

Here, Bentham is clearly influenced by Leibniz's theory of evil. For Leibniz, God allows *le mal moral*, moral evil, only because he knows that at some point in the future it will give rise to an incomparably greater good, a good that, in the absence of this evil, would not have come about. Thus, for instance, God permitted the crime of Sextus because he knew that this crime would serve 'for great things': it was precisely this crime that led to the founding of a great empire which provided mankind with 'noble examples'.[2] If this crime had not taken place, the greater good itself – the great empire, noble examples – would also not have occurred; and the moment 'the smallest evil that comes to pass in the world were missing in it, it would no longer be this world'.[3] God, then, permits the crimes of intelligent creatures to the extent that these crimes cause the good in this world to surpass evil to the greatest degree possible – that is to say, God permits the crimes to the extent that it is precisely *because of* these crimes that the created world is the best of all possible worlds. A world that would simply be good would of course have been better than the best possible world – but such a world is inherently impossible.

The same reasoning Leibniz used for justifying the existence of one of the three species of evil, i.e. crime, is used by Bentham to justify *punishment* for crimes. What exactly do we achieve by punishment? By means of punishment, which is in itself evil – punishment destroys some of the punished individual's happiness, and thus the overall happiness of the community is reduced – others, that is those 'under temptation to offend',[4] are deterred from committing acts similar to those of the criminals, that is, acts that would reduce the overall happiness of the community to an even greater extent. And it is by preventing this greater evil that we have indirectly contributed to the greatest happiness of the greatest number. With punishment, then, it is by sacrificing part of the punished individual's happiness that we contribute to the greatest good of all others, to the greatest happiness of the greatest number. Thus for Leibniz as for Bentham, we contribute to a greater '*good* of the *second order*' by risking a lesser '*evil* of the *first order*'; however, if for both Leibniz and Bentham, crime is evil, for Bentham it is also the *punishment* of crime that is evil.

In Bentham's eyes, the punishment itself is less intended for the punished, i.e. the guilty person, than it is for everyone else, i.e. the innocent: when Bentham weighs the value of reformation against that of setting an example – as the two principal objectives of punishment – he unequivocally opts for the latter: the setting of an example outweighs reformation, 'and that in the proportion of the number of the yet innocent to that of the convicted guilty'.[5] Moreover of all the objectives of punishment, example is 'beyond comparison the most important'.[6] Reformation is aimed at a comparatively small number of individuals – that is, at those who have already offended – whereas the setting of an example is aimed at all those 'exposed to the temptation of offending', and the number of the latter according to Bentham is, simply, 'the whole number of individuals of which the several political communities are composed – in other words, all mankind'.[7]

In Bentham's eyes, punishment is first and foremost a spectacle: it is insofar as punishment is not intended for the punished individual, but for all others, that the execution of the punishment is a spectacle. The dimension of spectacle in punishment therefore stems from the deterrent theory of punishment itself.

> It is the idea only of the punishment (or, in other words, the *apparent* punishment) that really acts upon the mind; the punishment itself (the *real* punishment) acts not any farther than as giving rise to that idea. It is the apparent punishment, therefore, that does all the service, I mean in the way of example, which is the principal object. It is the real punishment that does all the mischief.[8]

First, what exactly is punishment? Suffering, the experience of pain or loss of pleasure. The paradox of Bentham's punishment, which is intended for all the others rather than for the punished individual, is therefore evident: in punishment, it is only the punished individual (that is, the one for whom the punishment is not intended) who suffers pain, whereas the punishment acts upon all others (those for whom it is specifically intended) exclusively through its external appearance. This means that *appearance* (apparent punishment, apparent suffering) outweighs *reality* (real punishment, real suffering) whenever the number of the innocent exceeds one. The principal object of punishment, the deterrence of the innocent, is therefore achieved by means of appearance itself, that is, by raising the idea of punishment in the minds of the innocent. The key question then becomes: how is this appearance to be created?

Wherein exactly does this dimension of spectacle in punishment lie? What is it that is staged in punishment? Bentham's main concern here is in achieving the greatest apparent suffering with the least real suffering, that is, achieving the greatest effect of the punishment on others with the least inflicted pain.

Since it is only apparent punishment that acts upon others, upon their minds, it is not necessary, in order to increase the effect of punishment on others, to supplement the real punishment with some 'additional real punishment' – the same effect on others can be achieved by 'other less expensive means', namely, by staged 'solemnities distinct from punishment itself, and accompanying the execution of it'.[9]

Let us take a brief look at the characteristic features of punishment *qua* spectacle, features clearly intended for the innocent rather than for the punished, features that constitute the stage effect of the punishment.

Those who will later take an active part in the spectacle must first themselves be subjected to the spectacle; consequently, reception of prisoners into the panopticon prison resembles, as Janet Semple has remarked, 'an initiation ceremony rather than a bath':[10]

> On reception . . . thorough cleansing in a warm bath – thorough
> visitation by the surgeon. . . . Clothing new from top to toe. . . .
> Ablution – regeneration – solemnity – ceremony – form of prayer:
> the occasion would be impressive. Grave music . . . psalmody at
> least, with the organ.[11]

Prisoners in the panopticon would wear masks, the grimaces of the masks expressing the gravity of their offences: the prisoners would thus, as it were, stage their own guilt. They would wear these masks on 'the only occasion on which their eyes will have to encounter the public eye',[12] that is, during the divine service attended by outside worshippers. Since on this occasion the prisoners would know that they were exposed to public gaze, this 'perpetual pillory' could in time harden them and render them insensitive, ultimately impeding their reformation. On all other occasions, the prisoners would not know whether they were being watched, since the gaze of the public would be hidden from them: occasional visitors would only be allowed to look into the

panopticon from a central inspection tower which would allow
them to observe the prisoners while remaining invisible themselves.
Through the masks, then, guilt can be 'pilloried in the abstract'
without exposing the face of the guilty: at the same time, this
'masquerade', which is nonetheless 'serious, moving and instructive', heightens the salutary impression on the spectators. It is for
the gaze of the innocent – that is, for the gaze of those to be
deterred from offences – that the guilt of the prisoners in the
panopticon is staged.

In staging the spectacle of punishment, which is intended to be as
terrifying as possible, we can even draw upon the experience of the
Inquisition. It is true that the Inquisition's system of punishment was
unjust and barbaric, but the skills displayed by the Inquisitors in
producing the ultimate stage effect – their use of solemn processions,
emblematic clothing, terrifying scenery, etc. – in Bentham's eyes,
'deserve rather to be admired and imitated than condemned'.[13]

In the execution of punishment, which serves principally as
an example for the innocent, we must seize every opportunity to
fascinate their gaze: 'lose no occasion of speaking to the eye',[14]
writes Bentham. Thus, for Bentham, the key member of every
well-composed committee of penal law is none other than 'the
manager of a theatre'[15] who would, of course, know how to attain
the greatest effect from the staging of punishment.

The spectacle enables us to increase the magnitude of the apparent suffering without increasing the magnitude of the real suffering
involved. Thus, to attain the greatest effect of punishment on
others, it is not necessary to inflict additional, excessive pain on the
punished individual.

Whenever an equal effect of punishment on others can be achieved
by more economical means, every *additional* real punishment is
a pure loss, says Bentham. And *real* punishment, *real* suffering itself
– is it not also entirely superfluous?

Strictly speaking, the punished individual does not deserve
punishment, that is, pain; it is no less absurd to say that he deserves
pain than to say that he would deserve the smart of the surgeon's
cut if he were ill: 'No man *deserves* punishment', says Bentham.
'When a surgeon cuts into a limb, is it because the patient has
deserved the smart? No, but that the limb may be healed.'[16]
Furthermore, it would be equally absurd to expect that it is possible
to compensate for the offence itself through punishment, that is to

say, that the real suffering of the punished offender could bring adequate satisfaction to the victim of the offence. At the sight of the offender experiencing pain – no matter how horrific – the victim is bound to be disappointed and dissatisfied: according to Bentham, it is impossible through punishment, i.e. through pain experienced by the punished offender, to induce in the injured party a pleasure equivalent to the pain he has suffered as the victim of the offence.[17]

It might seem, then, that nothing can be achieved through *reality* that cannot be achieved as well through *appearance*.

If the principal object of punishment, the deterrence of others, can be achieved by means of appearances ('it is the apparent punishment that does all the service'), and if reality is entirely superfluous and even obstructive ('it is the real punishment that does all the mischief'), is it not then possible to achieve the same effect through *feigned* punishment, through fiction? In this way it would be possible to contribute to the overall happiness of the community without the slightest expense, without needing to sacrifice any of the punished individual's happiness.

For example, a building could be constructed resembling the panopticon from the outside; occasional screams, not of prisoners, but of people hired specifically for that purpose, could be heard from within. While the others would think that the offenders were being punished for their deeds, in truth, nobody at all would really be suffering punishment. A 'good of the second order' could then be produced without requiring any 'evil of the first order'.

Since the promotion of Benthamite ends through fallacy or illusion, or, more precisely, through an appearance which is not itself an effect of reality – in a word, through *fiction* – is actually counter-productive, as Ross Harrison puts it, 'the best, that is the easiest, surest, cheapest way of achieving the *appearance* of punishment, is by having the *real thing*',[18] i.e. the real panopticon. Bentham's objection to the unwarranted use of fictions is that it fosters disrespect for truth; fictions are only acceptable when they are indispensable.

However, even if we were to build a real panopticon, and even if we thus were to produce the appearance by means of reality, we still could not entirely avoid relying on fiction. This is because the panopticon, *reality itself, is already structured like a fiction*. For the real panopticon to achieve its *external* objective (the deterrence of the innocent from offending) – and this objective outweighs the processing of prisoners to the same extent as the number of the innocent exceeds the number of prisoners – it must of course first achieve its *internal* objective: it must deter the prisoners themselves from transgressing. But what deters the prisoners from transgressing, what sustains the panopticon in its internal structure, and lends the real thing its internal consistency, is, in fact, nothing other than a fiction.

Although the panopticon deters the innocent from committing offences by producing an appearance through reality, in order for this reality to be able to produce such an appearance at all, it must itself be sustained by another appearance, one that is not the effect of reality, but that is itself a fiction. If we were to remove this fiction from reality, we would lose reality itself.

III   FICTION IN THE PANOPTICON

Let us now examine to what extent the panopticon, as a *penal* institution, is, in its internal structure, a stage effect, a fiction.

According to Bentham, in the panopticon prison 'the *apparent omnipresence* of the inspector' is combined with 'the extreme facility of his *real presence*'.[19] It is precisely the inspector's apparent omnipresence that sustains perfect discipline in the panopticon, that deters the prisoners themselves from transgressing.

The oppositions – *real presence/apparent omnipresence*, *real punishment/apparent punishment* and *real suffering/apparent suffering* – invite comparison. According to Bentham, both the innocent and the prisoners are deterred through appearance – the former through *apparent* punishment, and the latter through the inspector's *apparent* omnipresence. The relation between appearance and reality is not, however, the same in both cases.

We have already seen how, for Bentham, appearance is related to reality in punishment: in punishment, the appearance is created in the innocent's mind by the real thing, by real punishment. The appearance is maximized, since the real thing has previously been minimized; real punishment, real suffering, has been minimized because it is in itself evil, and not because it hinders the production of the appearance, or, in other words, not because it would be impossible to produce the idea of punishment in the minds of the innocent with real punishment. Real punishment or suffering is perfectly capable of producing, as *its own appearance*, apparent punishment or suffering.

With the other pair of opposites, *real presence/apparent omnipresence*, however, the relation between appearance and reality is fundamentally different. Let us see what Bentham says. The moment the inspector allows himself to be seen anywhere in the panopticon he loses his omnipresence in the eyes of those who see him: those who see him, can, of course, tell whether his eyes are directed toward them; those who see him thus can see that they are not being seen. In this case, the inspector's apparent omnipresence is preserved only in the eyes of those who do not see him: since they do not see him anywhere in the panopticon, they clearly cannot see that they are not being seen; accordingly, they assume that he is present elsewhere in his station, from whence he may in fact be watching them, while he himself remains invisible.[20]

The relation between the inspector's apparent omnipresence and his real presence is then as follows: the less the inspector is really present, the more he is apparently omnipresent; or, more precisely, the inspector is *apparently omnipresent precisely insofar as he is not really present*, since a momentary exposure to the eyes of the prisoners is sufficient for him to lose his apparent omnipresence. Here, then, appearance *precludes* reality.

The panopticon is thus not an ordinary prison, in which the warden as a rule exposes himself to the eyes of the prisoners as much as possible precisely because he knows that the discipline of the prisoners depends on his real presence. Ordinary prisons generally present the following image: when the warden is not around, the prisoners naturally laze about, but, the moment he comes into sight, they stage work, order and discipline for his gaze. In Bentham's panopticon prison, however, the opposite is true: prisoners work dutifully as long as the inspector is not in view; in his presence, they stage, as it were, indiscipline, idleness and disorder. Thus, in the panopticon, the inspector exposes himself to the eyes of the prisoners as little as possible: all of his power over the prisoners derives from his invisibility, or more precisely, his 'invisible omnipresence'.[21]

The inspector's real presence, then, cannot produce the idea of his omnipresence in the minds of the prisoners in the same way as real punishment produced the idea of punishment in the minds of the innocent. While real punishment is perfectly capable of producing, as its own appearance, the idea of punishment, the only real thing or reality capable of producing the idea of omnipresence, as its own appearance, is God.

Bentham's own example shows just how strong his belief was that the only adequate appearance is the one produced by the real thing or reality itself as its own appearance. In other words, he held that *it is the thing itself that is its own most adequate appearance, its own most adequate representation*. When, shortly before his death, he was considering what he could leave his disciples to remember him by, he understandably did not choose a portrait, a bust or a death-mask; rather, he must have concluded that *there is nothing that could represent Jeremy Bentham more adequately than Jeremy Bentham himself*. A particular thing can most adequately be represented only by itself: therefore, each thing should be *its own icon*, that is an *auto-icon*. Accordingly, in his will, he requested that his body be dissected; that his disciples gather for the dissection of his body and listen to a final oration, given by the anatomist who performed the dissection, on the utility of dissecting dead bodies; that they should then preserve the body, dress it in his clothes, put his walking stick in its hand and his straw hat on its head, and sit it on his usual chair. And indeed Bentham's last wish came true. Thus, Bentham can still be seen today: he sits in a glass case in the hall of University College London, *representing himself*. A curious irony had it that the preservation of the body failed at the head – precisely the point by which it is possible to determine whether Bentham's corpse adequately represents Bentham himself, whether Bentham's body really is an auto-icon – the preserved head was markedly dissimilar to the head of the living Bentham. Since Bentham, then, no longer resembled himself and was no longer his own icon, his head had to be replaced by a wax replica. The irony of this lies not only in the fact that it was the example of Bentham himself that proved that the real thing is not necessarily its own most adequate representation, but also in the fact that the anatomist who performed the dissection could have consulted a treatise describing in detail the procedures of head-shrinking among the Maori, written by Bentham himself.[22]

In the eyes of the prisoners, the inspector is also endowed with other divine attributes: apart from being omnipresent, he is also all-seeing, omniscient and omnipotent. However, there is no reality that could produce, as its own appearance, the corresponding ideas in the minds of the prisoners. And it is precisely for this reason that the role of fiction in deterring the prisoners from transgressing, that is, the role of fiction *in* the panopticon, differs radically from the role of fiction in deterring the innocent from offences *through* the panopticon as an example. What has to be staged in the panopticon for the gaze of the prisoners is reality itself, i.e. God. Whereas the innocent are deterred from offending by real punishment, by the real suffering of the punished, the prisoners in the panopticon are deterred from transgressing by the *fiction of God*. It is therefore the fiction of God that sustains the universe of the panopticon. This deterrence of the prisoners in the panopticon from transgressing is unquestionably an example of the Benthamite end, which Bentham himself promotes through fallacy or illusion, through an appearance which is not itself an effect of reality – in a word, through fiction. And therein lies the ultimate stage effect of Bentham's panopticon: it creates the fiction of God with all his attributes.

IV   GAZE AND VOICE IN THE PANOPTICON

Bentham creates the fiction of God in the panopticon through a gaze and a voice. What sort of gaze and what sort of voice are at work? In the panopticon, we are seen without seeing the one who sees us; we hear a voice without seeing the one who speaks. The panopticon is governed by a gaze and a voice which are desubjectivized, detached from their bearer – in a word, by gaze and voice *qua* objects.

With this, the first step in the construction of God is taken. A gaze and a voice that cannot be pinned down to any particular bearer tend to acquire exceptional powers, and by themselves, as it were, constitute divine attributes.

In the panopticon, gaze and voice are produced by two devices so stunningly simple that it could even be said that the God constituted by them, the God of the panopticon, is perhaps nothing more than an inevitable by-product of putting this 'simple idea in architecture'[23] into effect. There is perhaps no other work of human hands, no icon, that can bring God closer to us, through which God can reveal himself to a greater extent than through Bentham's panopticon, although the God of the panopticon nevertheless always remains *Deus absconditus*, a God who jealously hides his face.

Let us first take a look at the voice in the panopticon. It is precisely to the exceptional status of his voice that the inspector owes his divine attributes: the panopticon is governed by a voice that – like the voice in films (most often represented by a voice on the telephone) that is not part of the diegetic reality and that therefore does not belong to anyone within the universe of the film – cannot be attached to any particular person within the universe of the panopticon. This bodiless voice is a perfect example of what Michel Chion calls *la voix acousmatique*. According to Chion, a voice whose source is invisible is automatically assigned exceptional powers: in our eyes, such a voice is, as a rule, endowed with divine attributes. It is as though its every word were a word coming directly from God. This bodiless, unlocatable voice functions as a shapeless threat lurking everywhere in the background. In our eyes, further-more, the bearer of this unseen voice himself sees everything: no one is more likely to see us and everything that we do not see than the one whom we ourselves do not see. The voice is thus possessed of divine attributes – it is omnipresent and all-seeing – as long as it remains unseen; the moment the voice finds its body, it loses the attributes. The bearer of this voice, who in our eyes has acquired exceptional powers, most often turns out to be nothing more than a powerless, vulnerable creature just like ourselves.[24]

The bodiless *voix acousmatique* is sustained in the panopticon by a device which, like the telephone, enables us to hear the voice with-out revealing the one who is speaking. The inspector communicates with the prisoners in their cells by means of 'conversation tubes' through which his voice is transmitted from the lodge into each indi-vidual cell.[25] In this way, the inspector is able to issue commands, instructions, warnings, etc., to the prisoners, without having to leave his post. He is able to speak to them without having to expose himself to the eyes of the prisoners; the prisoners can hear him, but they cannot see him. He is able to communicate with each of the prisoners individually without the others knowing. Since no one, except for the prisoner being addressed, can know whom the inspector is addressing at any given moment, it is obvious that no one can know for sure that he himself is not at that time under surveillance. Although all the inspector's attention is focused on the one prisoner to whom he is talking, none of the others can be certain that the inspector's eyes are not at that moment directed towards them.

Let us now turn to the role of the gaze in the panopticon. In the panopticon, the gaze is produced by the 'inspection-lantern', a device introduced in the *Postscript* I as a solution to the dilemma that Bentham faced in the *Letters* regarding the inspector's lodge. Because the prison-keeper in the panopticon is also the book-keeper, Bentham faces a dilemma, which could be termed 'the Prison-keeper's Dilemma': if, on the one hand, there were enough light in the lodge for the inspector to manage the books, he could not effectively perform his invisible inspection, since he would then be visible from the cells; if, on the other hand, there were not enough light for him to be visible from the cells, he could certainly perform his inspection, but would then be unable to keep his books.[26] The lantern, which would resolve this dilemma, has the shape of two short-necked funnels joined together at their necks; it is pierced in certain places, and pieces of coloured or smoked glass, through which the inspector looks, are inserted in the holes; the lantern is just big enough for the inspector to see everything around him without having to move from this spot – a turn of the head or body is sufficient. Owing to these numerous apertures, the lantern cannot entirely prevent light from passing through it, but is translucent, so that the inspector's body within it is to a certain degree discernible – from the cells he is visible as a silhouette, a shadow, or an opaque, dark spot.

Now of course there is a difficulty in this: if the inspector is omnipresent only insofar as he is invisible, and if he is all-seeing only insofar as he is himself not seen, does his partial visibility in any way weaken his supposed omnipresence and limit his all-seeing gaze? By no means, argues Bentham. The inspector's partial visibility in the translucent lantern does not allow the prisoner to determine whether the eye of the inspector is at that moment directed towards him any more than he can if the inspector is not at all visible. In this case, the inspector's partial visibility is equivalent to invisibility; his omni-presence is in no way affected, his gaze is still all-seeing, since the prisoner cannot see that he is not seen. All that the prisoner can see inside the lantern is an opaque, dark spot which is always gazing back at him.

Thus 'the Prison-keeper's Dilemma' is solved: in the lantern there is enough light for the inspector to keep the books, yet he is – despite his partial visibility – no less invisible than he would be if he were spying on the prisoners, hidden in the depths of a completely dark lodge. In neither case can the prisoners determine with certainty that they are not being watched at any particular moment; the only difference is that, in the former case, they are led to believe that the inspector is watching them from the lantern even when, in truth, he is completely absorbed in his books.

In constructing God by means of the illusion of the all-seeing gaze, Bentham was not without predecessors: Nicholas of Cusa had already put forward similar ideas in his 1453 treatise, *De visione Dei sive de icona*. Nicholas of Cusa sent to the monks at Tegernsee a portrait which was so cunningly painted that the viewer, from wherever he looked at it, got the impression that the figure in the picture was gazing back at him. To demonstrate the exceptional qualities of the picture, he suggested the following experiment. The painting is hung on a wall, and the monks gather in a semi-circle around it. Each of the monks then come to believe that the figure in the painting is looking back only at him and not at any of the others. In order to convince the monks that the figure in the picture is at the same time gazing at *all of them simultaneously*, that despite its immobility it is also capable of following them with its gaze and that therefore its gaze is all-seeing, one monk is instructed to trace a semi-circular path, with his eyes constantly on the picture, in one direction, while another monk does this in the opposite direction. Since they – each individually and both at the same time – will be left with the impression that the painted gaze is following them all the time, *visus iconae*, the gaze of the picture must therefore be all-seeing. Nicholas of Cusa suggested this experiment as the first step on the path to mystical theology, as an insight that would transport us beyond the visible, into the divine darkness: in short, as the first step on the path that culminates in the insight that I exist because God is looking at me and that the moment God turns his gaze away from me, I will cease to exist.[27]

For Nicholas of Cusa, only the illusion of the all-seeing gaze of the picture can be considered to be the representation of God. The unrepresentable, invisible God simply cannot be represented other than by *painting the gaze itself*, which is, from wherever we look at the picture, always directed back towards us. It is possible to comprehend God only by means of such a gaze, God is 'visible' only in such a gaze: in a word, God *is* the gaze itself. Every picture that creates the illusion of an all-seeing gaze – regardless of what it portrays, whether it is an image of Christ, an angel or a self-portrait of the painter – thus discloses God and can be called an 'icon of God'. Although this amounts to the declaration that a product of human hands is an icon of God, we cannot be reproached for idolatry, since, strictly speaking, what we worship is not the idol itself, but the elusive gaze.

While Bentham would perhaps agree with Nicholas of Cusa that God, 'that invisible and mysterious being',[28] can only become manifest in and as an all-seeing gaze, he would most likely object to the idea that every picture that produces the illusion of an all-seeing gaze could be said to be an icon of God: according to Bentham, no picture, no icon, but only God himself, can be said to be an icon of God. The lantern in the panopticon could thus be considered to be an icon of God only if the dark spot contained in it could be said to be God.

The same effect that Nicholas of Cusa characterized through an 'icon of God' is characterized by Bentham through the spot in the visual field, 'in the picture', the spot that gazes back at us. Bentham's version of the icon is three-dimensional, and the congregation is assembled around it in a full circle; in the panopticon, however, in contrast to Cusa's monks, movement is impossible, since the members of the congregation are chained to one point, as it were. This means that it is not possible to ascertain whether the gaze of the spot in the lantern is all-seeing by the same means that it was possible to determine that the gaze of the painting is all-seeing. To establish whether Bentham's lantern itself deserves the name 'icon of God' – that is, whether the spot in it constitutes God – an incomparably more subtle stratagem will be required.

V   AN UTTERLY DARK SPOT

How is it then possible, according to Bentham, to determine whether the gaze of the spot is all-seeing? In other words, how do we produce in the prisoners' minds the impression of the inspector's invisible omnipresence and the idea of constant surveillance? How does the inspector's gaze become all-seeing in the eyes of the prisoners? How do we elevate the inspector to the stature of God in the eyes of the prisoners? In short, how, according to Bentham, do we construct God?

The ideal situation in the panopticon prison would require that each prisoner should actually be under the inspector's eye 'during every instant of time'; since this is virtually impossible, 'the next thing to be wished for is, that, at every instant, seeing reason to believe as much, and not being able to satisfy himself to the contrary, he should *conceive* himself to be so',[29] writes Bentham. What is then staged in the panopticon is the illusion of constant surveillance: the prisoners are not really always under surveillance, they just think or imagine that they are.

The prisoner who does not see the inspector – because, in fact, their eyes never meet – of course cannot see that he is not seen. He can, however, attempt to find out whether the inspector's hidden, invisible eye is in fact always directed toward him, that is to say, whether the inspector's gaze is really all-seeing, whether the inspector is really omniscient.

How is it possible to determine when exactly the invisible eye, that is, the eye which is, as Jacques-Alain Miller puts it, 'looking at me even when it does not see me',[30] does not in fact see me? I first hazard, entirely at random, a less serious, still pardonable transgression; if this transgression goes unnoticed, I commit another, this time more serious, transgression. I can, of course, exploit this sort of discovery. According to Bentham, however, such attempts can be prevented in advance, once and for all – and in a single move.

> I will single out one of the most untoward of the prisoners. I will keep an unintermitted watch upon him. I will watch until I observe a transgression. I will minute it down. I will wait for another: I will note that down too. I will lie by for a whole day: he shall do as he pleases that day, so long as he does not venture at something too serious to be endured. The next day I produce the list to him. – *You thought yourself undiscovered: you abused my indulgence: see how you were mistaken. Another time, you may have rope for two days, ten days: the longer it is, the heavier it will fall upon you. Learn from this, all of you, that in this house transgression never can be safe.*[31]

Of course, only one action of this sort is needed for the inspector to appear all-seeing in the eyes of the prisoners: from this moment on, every prisoner will think that he himself is constantly under the gaze of the inspector, and that none of his movements can escape the ever wakeful, watchful eye of the inspector. Even if the inspector no longer keeps a list of further transgressions, even if he never again intervenes, even if he no longer watches, no longer surveys, the prisoners will now begin to do this by themselves: each will watch himself, each will keep in his mind a list of his own transgressions and calculate the gravity of the punishment that he will sooner or later have to suffer for them. The result of this is that, from this moment on, in the eyes of a prisoner who has committed a transgression and has not been immediately punished for it, the *absence of the inspector's intervention* – which can now easily be a consequence of the latter's inattention – will be interpreted as a *deferral of the inevitable punishment*. Although the inspector may completely abandon surveillance, from this moment on, each prisoner will believe that the inspector is preying upon him – whereas in truth, each prisoner is only preying upon himself. Thus, discipline is internalized, while the inspector himself has become superfluous. In this way, then, the impression of the inspector's invisible omnipresence and the idea of constant surveillance are produced in prisoners' minds. Thus, through the illusion of the all-seeing gaze of the dark spot in the lantern, God has been constructed and, in a single move, the last of the sceptics has been, as it were, converted. There can now no longer be any doubt: in the eyes of the subjects of the universe of the panopticon, the gaze of the dark spot *is* the all-seeing gaze of God, the spot in the lantern *is* God himself. Like any God worthy of the name, the inspector may, from this moment on, turn his back on the universe of the panopticon and peacefully devote himself to his book-keeping; from now on, the universe of the panopticon is perfectly capable of running without him.

The inspector's gaze is also all-seeing in another sense, that is in the sense that the inspector can see *more than is actually visible*. Since not all cells are equally visible from each storey of the central inspection tower, some of the prisoners are occasionally invisible to the inspector's eye; however, there is no cell of which at least some part is not visible from every storey of the inspection tower. To ensure that the cells that are not entirely visible from every storey are subject to the same surveillance as those cells that are entirely transparent from this point of view, a line is to be drawn on the floor of these cells, a line separating, in the eyes of the inspector, the prisoner's visibility from his invisibility: the prisoner is visible if he does not cross the line, whereas, once he has crossed the line, he becomes invisible. Invisibility is, no less than visibility, a reliable indicator of the prisoner's exact location at the time. Thus, if at a certain moment the prisoner cannot be seen, in the 'compact microcosm' of the panopticon, he can only be beyond the line. In the panopticon, it is impossible to escape the inspector's gaze even if the prisoners hide from his eyes and make themselves invisible – since once the prisoner has crossed the line and becomes invisible, 'his very invisibility is a mark to note him by',[32] writes Bentham. In the all-transparent, light-flooded universe of the panopticon, invisibility itself has become a positive quality, a *visible sign* of the prisoner, as it were. Thus, the inspector is in fact all-seeing: his gaze extends *beyond the limits of the visible into the invisible*.

According to Bentham, literally anything can constitute the spot that returns the prisoners' gaze. Since the lantern is translucent, the prisoners can of course see from their cells whether the inspector is present in it; in other words, if the inspector were absent, the prisoners would see that they were not being watched at that moment. Therefore, the inspector disguises his absence (he leaves the lantern surreptitiously: he lets himself out through a trap-door in the floor and descends through the interior of the central tower) by placing 'any opaque object'[33] in the lantern. The difference between an inanimate object, constantly at rest, and the inspector's body, occasionally in motion, would not be discernible, according to Bentham, because the apertures in the lantern are so small. At this point, what constitutes the spot that returns the prisoners' gaze, what sustains the all-seeing gaze, is nothing more than an opaque object. Regardless of what it is that constitutes the spot in the lantern – the inspector's body or an opaque object – the prisoners will always believe that they are under constant surveillance.

The prisoners in the panopticon are 'awed to silence by an invisible eye', yet what is gazing back at them is not necessarily a pair of eyes nor the inspector himself, but whatever happens to constitute the utterly dark spot in the transparent lantern. What is staged in the panopticon is therefore the all-seeing gaze itself. The lantern may then be said to be a device for *reproducing an all-seeing gaze*. From whichever cell on the circumference of the panopticon the prisoner looks at the lantern, an utterly dark spot will always gaze back at him, the inspector's eye will at every moment be directed precisely towards him. In Bentham's words, 'in a Panopticon the inspector's back is never turned'.[34]

VI   GOD AS A NON-ENTITY

God is thus produced, with all of his attributes, in a way similar
to the famous scene described by Hitchcock, in which a corpse is
'produced' through assembling an automobile:

> I wanted to have a long dialogue scene between Cary Grant and one
> of the factory workers [at a Ford automobile plant] as they walk
> along the assembly line. They might, for instance, be talking about
> one of the foremen. Behind them a car is being assembled, piece by
> piece. Finally, the car they've seen being put together from a simple
> nut and bolt is complete, with gas and oil, and all ready to drive off
> the line. The two men look at each other and say, 'Isn't it wonderful!'
> Then they open the door of the car and out drops a corpse.[35]

We would be no less surprised if we were to follow the construction
of Bentham's panopticon as it were assembled piece by piece before
our very eyes: although we would be watching the assembly of the
panopticon, not only would a building be produced, but also God
within it. The panopticon is perhaps really nothing more than 'a
simple idea in architecture',[36] as Bentham says, but if we were to
realize this idea by faithfully following Bentham's plan, we would
produce, so to speak, *at the same time as the building itself* – which
we have built out of bricks, iron, glass, etc. – *God as well*. We can
only regret that both Hitchcock's scene and Bentham's panopticon
remain ideas that were never realized by their authors.

In Bentham's eyes, the panopticon is a living entity, 'an artificial
body', which is kept alive by the inspector with his gaze and
his voice: 'the lodge is the heart, which gives life and motion to
this artificial body'.[37] The properties manifest in the functioning of
this artificial body are 'certainty, promptitude, and uniformity'; in
a word, the artificial body functions with 'clockwork regularity':
'action scarcely follows thought quicker than execution might here
be made to follow command'.[38]

Further, it seems that the inspector is more closely tied to this
artificial body than he is to his own body. While on the one hand
his own body is, so to speak, paralysed (the inspector does not
move and surveillance is carried out from one single point, so that
he is perhaps even more confined in his lantern than are the inmates
in their cells), on the other hand, with the help of the gaze produced
by the lantern and the voice produced by the conversation tubes
(representing the arteries and nerves of the artificial body), he is in

complete command of the artificial body. No detail of this body can escape the gaze of inspector: 'every motion of the [prisoners'] limbs, and every muscle of [their] face[s]'[39] is exposed to his view. He is, with regard to the artificial body of the panopticon, the realization of Spinozistic *omniscient anatomist*, who is aware of everything that goes on in his own body, down to the smallest detail. The inspector therefore more thoroughly inhabits and animates the artificial body, the panopticon, than his own body.

Without the inspector, who gives this artificial body motion and life with his surveillance, it would certainly die: without a God who sustains it with his all-seeing gaze and his 'unseen voice', this body would certainly collapse. In spite of this, however, the universe of the panopticon is not a Berkeleian universe and the God of the panopticon is not a Berkeleian God. For Berkeley, a universe without a God who always imagines it would cease to exist: the universe is, in a strict sense, a fiction in the imagination of God – if God were to stop imagining it, it would cease to exist. Similarly, it could be said that the universe of the panopticon only exists as long as it is sustained by the gaze of God. But there is a crucial difference between these two universes: for Bentham, the universe is not a fiction in God's imagination; rather, *God himself is a fiction in the imaginations of the subjects of this universe*. It is true that God is the one who sustains the universe with his gaze; but it is the subjects of this universe who imagine that this gaze really exists. The universe of the panopticon would thus disintegrate the moment that the prisoners stopped imagining God, or, more precisely, the moment that they stopped imagining the inspector as God – that is, the moment he lost his divine attributes.

Thus, although the God of the panopticon does not exist, he nevertheless has real effects; although he is merely a fiction in the imaginations of the prisoners, that is, an imaginary non-entity, without him the universe of the panopticon would collapse. It could even be said that the real effects of the God of the panopticon are a result of his ontological status as a fiction.

Both fictitious entities, which themselves do not exist, and imaginary non-entities, which are utterly unreal, can have all too real effects.[40]

As an example of the real effects of a fictitious entity, let us take the concept of a legal right, which is in Bentham's eyes an 'ethical fictitious entity'. Even though a particular legal right of mine does not actually exist as an entity, even though it is merely a so-called 'fictitious object', that is, an object whose existence is feigned in the imagination, others cannot act as if it did not exist; although in a strict sense I cannot be said actually to have it, others nevertheless cannot act as if I did not have it. For not acting in accordance with their duties in which my right is mirrored, others are threatened with punishment[41] – i.e. an experience of pain or loss of pleasure – and pain and pleasure are for Bentham real entities *par excellence*, i.e. 'perceptible real entities'. Thus, although a right does not actually exist as an entity, although its existence is merely feigned in the imagination, it nevertheless has real effects.

As an example of the real effects of imaginary non-entities, we can consider Bentham's fear of ghosts. In Bentham's elaborate ontology, ghosts – as well as hobgoblins, vampires, the devil, etc. – are classified as 'fabulous maleficent beings',[42] or, more precisely, imaginary non-entities. Ontologically, they are on the same level as God, who is considered by Bentham as 'a non-entity', rather than 'a superhuman inferential entity'.[43] Now even though Bentham classified ghosts as imaginary non-entities, even though he therefore did not believe in their existence, he was, in his own words, nevertheless, for his whole life, pathologically afraid of them.[44]

Bentham's attitude to ghosts is paradoxical:

> In no man's judgement can a stronger persuasion of the non-existence of these sources of terror have place than in mine; yet no sooner do I lay myself down to sleep in a dark room than, if no other person is in the room, and my eyes keep open, these instruments of terror obtrude themselves.[45]

Strictly speaking, it is probably the case that no one who is afraid of ghosts believes that they really exist; not only Bentham, but all of us most likely believe that ghosts are purely fictitious, mere figments of the imagination, but we are nevertheless still afraid of them.

But this is only an apparent paradox: we are not afraid of ghosts *in spite of the fact* that they do not exist, but precisely *because of the fact* that they do not exist. Of what, exactly, are we afraid when we say that we are afraid of ghosts? It is precisely the intrusion of something radically other, something unknown and strange into our world. And it is from this fear that we would escape, if we could be sure that ghosts *really existed*. Or, in the words of Paul

Veyne, who is himself 'almost neurotically afraid of them': 'nothing
would reassure me more than to learn that ghosts "really" exist'.[46]
In this case, we could deal with ghosts in the same way that we
deal with all other real entities; they would simply be phenomena
comparable with all others. Even if this would not completely do
away with our fear, even if we were still afraid of ghosts, we would
be afraid in a *different* way: we would then be afraid of ghosts
in the same way that we fear all the *real* entities that we naturally
designate as *maleficent*, like, for example, vicious dogs.

We can see that this is true if we try to shake off the fear of ghosts
by refuting their existence, that is, if we try to convince ourselves
that it is not true that ghosts exist and that therefore our fear is
unfounded. Clearly, the fear will by no means lessen; quite the
contrary, it will become even stronger. We might even say that the
most unbearable thing would be to succeed in refuting the existence
of ghosts. Bentham's own experience bears witness to the fact that
the refutation of the existence of ghosts cannot rid us of the fear of
them, that such an attempt only intensifies this fear, and that what
would really reassure us would be the certainty that ghosts do in
fact exist. Although every night before going to sleep, with the
intention of shaking off his fears, he rehearsed arguments refuting
the existence of ghosts,[47] as soon as he found himself alone in
the dark, he was inevitably seized by fear. He was seized by fear not
in spite of his arguments, but *because of* them. If the refutation of
the existence of ghosts could not reassure him, then it must not
have been the *existence* of ghosts that he feared; he must surely
have been afraid of something else. If Bentham was afraid of anything, then it could only have been of the *non-existence* of ghosts,
that is, of the fact that ghosts are imaginary non-entities. Thus
Bentham would probably have been able to go to sleep peacefully if
he could have been assured that ghosts *do in fact exist* and are not
mere fictions. In other words, only when he was sure that ghosts
really did exist could he start acting as if they did not.

The fear of ghosts is perhaps the purest example of how an
imaginary non-entity owes its real effects to its ontological status
as a fiction; if ghosts were not fictitious, if they were really
existing entities, then they would either not have any effects at all,
or they would have different effects.

Just like ghosts, the God of the panopticon also has effects
only as a fiction. If the 'hidden' God were to reveal himself in the

panopticon, if the apparent omnipresence of God in the eyes of the prisoners were replaced by the real presence of the inspector, a real entity comparable to themselves (that is, the utterly powerless inspector), he would then either cease to have any effect or would simply have different effects. If the real presence of the inspector still had effects on the prisoners, this presence would not be as effective in deterring them from transgressing as would the 'invisible omnipresence'. The inspector can sustain the smooth functioning of the panopticon prison only insofar as he appears to be God, that is, only insofar as he is, in the eyes of the prisoners, endowed with divine attributes (apparent omnipresence, an all-seeing gaze, etc.) – in a word, only insofar as he is a fiction in the imaginations of the prisoners. It is thus through his non-existence that God sustains the universe of the panopticon.

In Lacan, who often refers to Bentham's theory of fictions, we find an analogous argument in his account of the love of God. Just as we are afraid of ghosts and of the God of the panopticon insofar as they are imaginary non-entities – that is, because they do not exist – so, according to Lacan, we love God precisely because he does not exist. What we love in an object is precisely that which it lacks. But then what is it in God, who obviously lacks nothing, that we can love? In other words, if it is only giving what we do not have that counts as a sign of love, then is it even possible for God, who lacks nothing, to give anything at all? Since God simply has everything, he obviously has nothing that he could give. The only thing that God, who is supposed to be a total plenitude of being, could lack, is, as Lacan puts it, precisely the principal feature of being: existence. It is an illusion to think that we love God because he is a total plenitude of being; the only reason we love him is that perhaps he does not even exist at all.[48] If we love God, we love him because he is a non-entity.

The inspector certainly knows that, *qua* God, he does not really exist; *qua* God, the inspector only exists through an artifice, only as a fiction. Because he owes his divine attributes to his invisibility, he must always hide himself from the eyes of the prisoners; he lives in the constant fear that the prisoners will find out that he really does not exist. If Bentham's idea had been realized, if the panopticon prison had really been built, and if he would have become its inspector-manager – Bentham reserved the place of the dark spot, the place of God in the panopticon for himself – then he would, as later befell Louis Althusser, most likely himself fall victim to a fantasy of not existing. As Althusser says in his autobiography, *L'Avenir dure longtemps*, he believed he did not exist, or, more precisely, he believed he existed merely as a fiction in the imaginations of others; in Bentham's terms, he thought of himself merely as an imaginary non-entity. Althusser existed in the same way as Bentham's inspector, who exists *qua* God only through artifice, by adopting divine attributes: 'I was only able to exist through artifice, by adopting characteristics which were not my own',[49] Althusser said of himself. He had his books published in order to conceal the fact that he did not exist, and every time they were published he feared that others would see through his ruse. Moreover, in his own words, he wanted at all costs to destroy himself *because he had never existed*.[50] Since he existed solely as a fiction of others' imaginations, he was only able to destroy himself by destroying those whose fiction he believed himself to be; he began with the one person who most firmly believed in his existence.

Jacques-Alain Miller writes that the panopticon is nothing other than a 'materialized classification' or a classification 'inscribed in stone' – just as, on the other hand, the endless classifications, logical trees, divisions, tables, etc., which Bentham indefatigably elaborated, are only 'prisons of language' or 'prisons of words'.[51] Bentham undertook the elucidation of fictions so as not to leave the field of fictions 'in the state of an utterly *dark spot*',[52] or, more precisely, so that in the synoptic tables of entities, the field of fictions would not present itself 'to the eye of the mind in the repulsive character of an absolutely dark spot'.[53] And yet, by creating God in the panopticon, he himself thus created a fiction in the form of an utterly dark spot.

A NOTE ON THE TEXTS

Panopticon Letters and selections from *Panopticon Postscript* I are reprinted from volume IV, and *Fragment on Ontology* from volume VIII of the Bowring edition of *The Works of Jeremy Bentham* (11 vols, Edinburgh 1838–43). The panopticon writings have not yet appeared in the modern scholarly edition *The Collected Works of*

Jeremy Bentham, general eds J.H. Burns, J.R. Dinwiddy, and F. Rosen (London and Oxford 1968–) which is still in progress.

NOTES

1. Jeremy Bentham, *An Introduction to the Principles of Morals and Legislation* (Buffalo: Prometheus Books, 1988), 170.
2. G.W. Leibniz, *Theodicy*, trans. E.M. Huggard (La Salle, Illinois: Open Court, 1988), 373.
3. *Ibid.*, 128–9.
4. Bentham, *An Introduction*, 171, n.
5. Bentham, *Panopticon: Postscript* I, in *The Works of Jeremy Bentham*, ed. J. Bowring, Edinburgh 1838–43, vol. IV, 79, n. (99). (The additional number in brackets indicates the page in the present volume.)
6. Bentham, *Panopticon versus New South Wales*, Bowring IV, 174.
7. *Ibid.*
8. Bentham, *An Introduction*, 193 (Bentham's emphasis).
9. *Ibid.*
10. Janet Semple, *Bentham's Prison: A Study of the Panopticon Penitentiary* (Oxford: Clarendon Press, 1993), 122.
11. Bentham, *Panopticon: Postscript* II, Bowring IV, 158.
12. Bentham, *Panopticon: Postscript* I, 79, n. (99).
13. *Ibid.* (100).
14. *Ibid.*, 80, n. (100).
15. *Ibid.* (100).
16. Bentham, *Plan for Parliamentary Reform*, Bowring III, 533; quoted in Ross Harrison, *Bentham* (London: Routledge & Kegan Paul, 1985), 234 (Bentham's emphasis).
17. Bentham, *An Introduction*, 171, n. 1.
18. Harrison, *Bentham*, 235; see also 219 (emphasis added).
19. Bentham, *Panopticon: Letters*, Bowring IV, 45 (45; Bentham's emphasis).
20. Bentham, *Panopticon: Postscript* I, 83 and 89 (108).
21. Bowring XI, 96; quoted in John Dinwiddy, *Bentham* (Oxford: Oxford University Press, 1989), 92.
22. For a vivid description of the dissection, see Harrison, *Bentham*, 1–23.
23. Bentham, *Panopticon: Preface*, Bowring IV, 39 (31).
24. Michel Chion, *La voix au cinéma* (Paris: Cahiers du Cinéma/Editions de l'Etoile, 1982), 25–33.
25. Bentham, *Panopticon: Letters*, 41 (36–7).
26. Bentham, *Panopticon: Postscript* I, 80 (101).

27. Nicholas of Cusa, *The Vision of God*, trans. E. Gurney-Salter, in *The Portable Medieval Reader*, ed. J.B. Ross and M.M. McLaughlin (Harmondsworth: Penguin Books, 1978), 682–6.

28. Bentham, *A Fragment on Ontology*, Bowring VIII, 196, n. (119).

29. Bentham, *Panopticon: Letters*, 40 (34; Bentham's emphasis).

30. Jacques-Alain Miller, 'Le despotisme de l'Utile: la machine panoptique de Jeremy Bentham', *Ornicar?* 3 (May 1975), 5.

31. Bentham, *Panopticon: Postscript* I, 81–2, n. (104; Bentham's emphasis).

32. *Ibid.*, 71.

33. *Ibid.*, 82 (105).

34. *Ibid.*, 96.

35. François Truffaut, *Hitchcock* (London: Panther, 1969), 321.

36. Bentham, *Panopticon: Preface*, 39 (31).

37. Bentham, *Panopticon: Postscript* I, 83–4 (108).

38. *Ibid.*, 85 (111).

39. Bentham, *Panopticon: Letters*, 47 (49).

40. Fictitious entities do not exist, but not in the same way that non-entities do not exist, for fictitious entities have 'a sort of verbal reality' (*Chrestomathia*, Bowring VIII, 126, n.) which non-entities do not have, and so, despite their qualifications as fictitious, are still called entities. On Bentham's distinction between fictitious entities and imaginary non-entities, see Harrison, *Bentham*, 77–105; Jacques Bouvresse, 'La théorie des fictions chez Bentham', in *Regards sur Bentham et l'utilitarisme: Actes du colloque organisé à Genève les 23 et 24 novembre 1990*, ed. Kevin Mulligan and Robert Roth (Geneva: Librairie Droz, 1993), 87–98; and Slavoj Žižek, *Tarrying with the Negative* (Durham: Duke University Press, 1993), 83–9.

41. Bentham, *A Fragment on Government*, ed. J.H. Burns and H.L.A. Hart (Cambridge: Cambridge University Press, 1988), 108, n.; see also *An Introduction*, 224, n. 1.

42. Quoted in C.K. Ogden, *Bentham's Theory of Fictions* (London: Kegan Paul, 1932), xiv.

43. Bentham, *A Fragment on Ontology*, 195–6 (119).

44. 'This subject of ghosts has been among the torments of my life. Even now, when sixty or seventy years have passed over my head since my boyhood received the impression which my grandmother gave it, though my judgement is wholly free, my imagination is not wholly so' (quoted in Ogden, *Bentham's Theory of Fictions*, xi). We can see just how strong Bentham's fear of ghosts was from the fact that in his eyes it was one of the principal arguments against prolonged solitary confinement: 'When the external senses are restrained from action, the imagination is more active, and produces a numerous race of ideal beings. In a state of solitude, infantine superstitions, ghosts, and spectres, recur to the imagination. This, of itself, forms a sufficient reason for not prolonging this species of

punishment, which may overthrow the powers of the mind, and produce incurable melancholy. . . . [I]f greatly prolonged, it would scarcely fail of producing madness, despair, or more commonly a stupid apathy' (Bowring I, 426; quoted in Semple, *Bentham's Prison*, 132). The panopticon solves this problem by constructing a paradoxical crowded solitude: every prisoner is literally 'alone in a crowd'.

45. Ogden, *Bentham's Theory of Fictions*, xvi.

46. Paul Veyne, *Did the Greeks Believe in their Myths?*, trans. Paula Wissing (Chicago: The University of Chicago Press, 1988), 87.

47. Ogden, *Bentham's Theory of Fictions*, xvi.

48. See Jacques Lacan, *Le Seminaire, livre* IV: *La relation d'objet* (Paris: Editions du Seuil, 1994), ch. 8.

49. Louis Althusser, *The Future Lasts a Long Time*, trans. Richard Veasey (London: Chatto & Windus, 1993), 93.

50. *Ibid.*, 277.

51. Miller, 'Le Despotisme de l'Utile', 19–20.

52. Bentham, *Chrestomathia*, 127, n. (Bentham's emphasis).

53. *Ibid.*, 119–20.

PANOPTICON;

OR,

THE INSPECTION-HOUSE:

CONTAINING THE

IDEA OF A NEW PRINCIPLE OF CONSTRUCTION

APPLICABLE TO

ANY SORT OF ESTABLISHMENT, IN WHICH PERSONS OF
ANY DESCRIPTION ARE TO BE KEPT UNDER INSPECTION;

AND IN PARTICULAR TO

PENITENTIARY-HOUSES,

PRISONS,	POOR-HOUSES,	LAZARETTOS,
HOUSES OF INDUSTRY,	MANUFACTORIES,	HOSPITALS,
WORK-HOUSES,	MAD-HOUSES,	AND SCHOOLS:

WITH

A PLAN OF MANAGEMENT

ADAPTED TO THE PRINCIPLE:

IN A SERIES OF LETTERS,

WRITTEN IN THE YEAR 1787, FROM CRECHEFF IN WHITE
RUSSIA, TO A FRIEND IN ENGLAND.

BY JEREMY BENTHAM,

OF LINCOLN'S INN, ESQUIRE.

CONTENTS

PANOPTICON,

or,

THE INSPECTION-HOUSE, &C.

PREFACE.

*Morals reformed – health preserved – industry invigorated –
instruction diffused – public burthens lightened – Economy
seated, as it were, upon a rock – the gordian knot of the Poor-
Laws are not cut, but untied – all by a simple idea in
Architecture!* —— Thus much I ventured to say on laying down
the pen – and thus much I should perhaps have said on taking
it up, if at that early period I had seen the whole of the way
before me. A new mode of obtaining power of mind over mind,
in a quantity hitherto without example: and that, to a degree
equally without example, secured by whoever chooses to have
it so, against abuse. – Such is the engine: such the work that
may be done with it. How far the expectations thus held out
have been fulfilled, the reader will decide.

The Letters which compose the body of this tract were
written at Crecheff in Russia, and from thence sent to England
in the year 1787, much about the same time with the DEFENCE
of USURY. They were addressed to a particular person, with
a view to a particular establishment then in contemplation
(intelligence of which had found its way to me through the
medium of an English newspaper), and without any immediate
or very determinate view to general publication. The attention
of the public in Ireland having been drawn to one of the subjects
to which they relate, by the notice given not long ago by
the Chancellor of the Exchequer, of a disposition on the part of

the government there, to make trial of the Penitentiary system, it is on that account that they now see the light through the medium of the Irish press.

They are printed as at first written, with no other alteration than the erasure of a few immaterial passages, and the addition of a Postscript, stating such new ideas as have been the fruit of a more detailed and critical examination, undertaken chiefly with an eye to the particular establishment last mentioned, and assisted by professional information and advice.

In running over the descriptive part of the letters, the reader will find it convenient to remember, that alterations, as stated in the Postscript, have been made, though he need not at that period trouble himself with considering what they are: since in either shape the details will serve equally well for the illustration of the general principle, and for the proof of the advantages that may be derived from it.

In what concerns the Penitentiary system, I may be observed to have discussed, with rather more freedom than may perhaps be universally acceptable, a variety of measures either established or proposed by gentlemen who have laboured in the same line. A task this, which I would gladly have avoided: but complete justice could not otherwise have been done to the plan here proposed, nor its title to preference placed in a satisfactory point of view. Among the notions thus treated, it is with pleasure rather than regret that I observe several which on a former occasion I had myself either suggested or subscribed to. I say with pleasure: regarding the incident as a proof of my having no otherwise done by others than as I not only would be done by, but have actually done by myself: a consideration which will, I hope, make my apology to the respectable gentlemen concerned, and assist their candour in recommending me to their forgiveness. If by the light of reciprocal animadversion I should find myself enabled to rectify any errors of my own which may still have escaped me, the correction, instead of being shrunk from as a punishment, will be embraced as a reward.

In point of method and compression, something might have been gained, had the whole, Letters and Postscript together, been new cast, and the supplemental matter worked up with the original. But time was wanting; and, if the invention be worth any thing, the account given of it will not be the less amusing or less instructive, for being exhibited in an historical and progressive point of view.

The concluding Letter on Schools is a sort of *jeu d'esprit*, which would hardly have presented itself in so light a form, at any other period than at the moment of conception, and under the flow of spirits which the charms of novelty are apt enough to inspire. As such, it may possibly help to alleviate the tedium of a dry discussion, and on that score obtain the pardon, should it fail of receiving the approbation, of the graver class of readers.

LETTER I.
IDEA OF THE INSPECTION PRINCIPLE.

Crecheff in White Russia,
— 1787.

DEAR ****, – I observed t'other day in one of your English papers, an advertisement relative to a HOUSE of CORRECTION therein spoken of, as intended for *******. It occurred to me, that the plan of a building, lately contrived by my brother, for purposes in some respects similar, and which, under the name of the *Inspection House*, or the *Elaboratory*, he is about erecting here, might afford some hints for the above establishment.*
I have accordingly obtained some drawings relative to it, which I here enclose. Indeed I look upon it as capable of applications of the most extensive nature; and that for reasons which you will soon perceive.

To say all in one word, it will be found applicable, I think, without exception, to all establishments whatsoever, in which, within a space not too large to be covered or commanded by buildings, a number of persons are meant to be kept under

---

* The sudden breaking out of the war between the Turks and Russians, in consequence of an unexpected attack made by the former on the latter, concurred with some other incidents in putting a stop to the design. The person here spoken of, at that time Lieutenant-Colonel Commandant of a battalion in the Empress's service, having obtained a regiment and other honours for his services in the course of the war, is now stationed with his regiment in a distant part of the country.

inspection. No matter how different, or even opposite the purpose: whether it be that of *punishing the incorrigible, guarding the insane, reforming the vicious, confining the suspected, employing the idle, maintaining the helpless, curing the sick, instructing the willing* in any branch of industry, or *training the rising race* in the path of *education*: in a word, whether it be applied to the purposes of *perpetual prisons* in the room of death, or *prisons for confinement* before trial, or *penitentiary-houses*, or *houses of correction*, or *work-houses*, or *manufactories*, or *mad-houses*, or *hospitals*, or *schools*.

It is obvious that, in all these instances, the more constantly the persons to be inspected are under the eyes of the persons who should inspect them, the more perfectly will the purpose of the establishment have been attained. Ideal perfection, if that were the object, would require that each person should actually be in that predicament, during every instant of time. This being impossible, the next thing to be wished for is, that, at every instant, seeing reason to believe as much, and not being able to satisfy himself to the contrary, he should *conceive* himself to be so. This point, you will immediately see, is most completely secured by my brother's plan; and, I think, it will appear equally manifest, that it cannot be compassed by any other, or to speak more properly, that if it be compassed by any other, it can only be in proportion as such other may approach to this.

To cut the matter as short as possible, I will consider it at once in its application to such purposes as, being most complicated, will serve to exemplify the greatest force and variety of precautionary contrivance. Such are those which have suggested the idea of *penitentiary-houses*: in which the objects of *safe custody, confinement, solitude, forced labour*, and *instruction*, were all of them to be kept in view. If all these objects can be accomplished together, of course with at least equal certainty and facility may any lesser number of them.

LETTER II.
PLAN FOR A PENITENTIARY INSPECTION-HOUSE.

BEFORE you look at the plan, take in words the general idea of it.

The building is circular.

The apartments of the prisoners occupy the circumference. You may call them, if you please, the *cells*.

These *cells* are divided from one another, and the prisoners by that means secluded from all communication with each other, by *partitions* in the form of *radii* issuing from the circumference towards the centre, and extending as many feet as shall be thought necessary to form the largest dimension of the cell.

The apartment of the inspector occupies the centre; you may call it if you please the *inspector's lodge*.

It will be convenient in most, if not in all cases, to have a vacant space or *area* all round, between such centre and such circumference. You may call it if you please the *intermediate* or *annular* area.

About the width of a cell may be sufficient for a *passage* from the outside of the building to the lodge.

Each cell has in the outward circumference, a *window*, large enough, not only to light the cell, but, through the cell, to afford light enough to the correspondent part of the lodge.

The inner circumference of the cell is formed by an iron *grating*, so light as not to screen any part of the cell from the inspector's view.

Of this grating, a part sufficiently large opens, in form of a *door*, to admit the prisoner at his first entrance; and to give admission at any time to the inspector or any of his attendants.

To cut off from each prisoner the view of every other, the partitions are carried on a few feet beyond the grating into the intermediate area: such projecting parts I call the *protracted partitions*.

It is conceived, that the light, coming in in this manner through the cells, and so across the intermediate area, will be sufficient for the inspector's lodge. But, for this purpose, both the windows in the cells, and those corresponding to them in the lodge, should be as large as the strength of the building, and what shall be deemed a necessary attention to economy, will permit.

To the windows of the lodge there are *blinds*, as high up as the eyes of the prisoners in their cells can, by any means they can employ, be made to reach.

To prevent *thorough light*, whereby, notwithstanding the blinds, the prisoners would see from the cells whether or no any person was in the lodge, that apartment is divided into quarters, by *partitions* formed by two diameters to the circle, crossing each other at right angles. For these partitions the thinnest materials might serve; and they might be made removeable at pleasure; their height, sufficient to prevent the prisoners seeing over them from the cells. Doors to these partitions, if left open at any time, might produce the thorough light. To prevent this, divide each partition into two, at any part required, setting down the one-half at such distance from the other as shall be equal to the aperture of a door.

These windows of the inspector's lodge open into the intermediate area, in the form of *doors*, in as many places as shall be deemed necessary to admit of his communicating readily with any of the cells.

Small *lamps*, in the outside of each window of the lodge, backed by a reflector, to throw the light into the corresponding cells, would extend to the night the security of the day.

To save the troublesome exertion of voice that might otherwise be necessary, and to prevent one prisoner from knowing that the inspector was occupied by another prisoner at a distance, a small *tin tube* might reach from each cell to the inspector's lodge, passing across the area, and so in at the side of the correspondent window of the lodge. By means of this implement, the slightest whisper of the one might be heard by the other, especially if he had proper notice to apply his ear to the tube.

With regard to *instruction*, in cases where it cannot be duly given without the instructor's being close to the work, or without setting his hand to it by way of example before the learner's face, the instructor must indeed here as elsewhere, shift his station as often as there is occasion to visit different workmen; unless he calls the workmen to him, which in some of the instances to which this sort of building is applicable, such as that of imprisoned felons, could not so well be. But in all cases where directions, given verbally and at a distance, are sufficient, these tubes will be found of use. They will save, on the one hand, the exertion of voice it would require, on the part of the instructor, to communicate instruction to the workmen without quitting his central station in the lodge; and, on the other, the confusion which would ensue if different instructors or persons in the lodge were calling to the cells at the same time. And, in the case of hospitals, the quiet that may be insured by this little contrivance, trifling as it may seem at first sight, affords an additional advantage.

A *bell*, appropriated exclusively to the purposes of *alarm*, hangs in a *belfry* with which the building is crowned, communicating by a rope with the inspector's lodge.

The most economical, and perhaps the most convenient, way of *warming* the cells and area, would be by flues surrounding it, upon the principle of those in hot-houses. A total want of every means of producing artificial heat might, in such weather as we sometimes have in England, be fatal to the lives of the prisoners; at any rate, it would often times be altogether incompatible with their working at any sedentary employment. The flues, however, and the fire-places belonging to them, instead of being on the outside, as in hot-houses, should be in the inside. By this means, there would be less waste of heat, and the current of air that would rush in on all sides through the cells, to supply the draught made by the fires, would answer so far the purpose of ventilation. But of this more under the head of Hospitals.*

---

* There is one subject, which, though not of the most dignified kind, nor of the most pleasant kind to expatiate upon, is of too great importance to health and safe custody to be passed over unconsidered: I mean the provision to be made for carrying off the result of necessary evacuations. A common necessary might be dangerous to security, and would be altogether incompatible with the plan of solitude. To have the filth carried off by the attendants, would be altogether as incompatible with cleanliness; since without such a degree of regularity as it would be difficult, if not ridiculous, to attempt to enforce in case of health, and altogether impossible in case of sickness, the air of each cell, and by that means the lodge itself would be liable to be kept in a state of constant contamination, in the intervals betwixt one visit and another. This being the case, I can see no other eligible means, than that of having in each cell a fixed provision made for this purpose in the construction of the building.

LETTER III.
EXTENT FOR A SINGLE BUILDING.

So far as to the characteristic parts of the principle of construction. You may now, perhaps, be curious to know to what extent a building upon this principle is capable of being carried, consistently with the various purposes to which it may come to be applied. Upon this subject, to speak with confidence belongs only to architects by profession. Indulge me, however, with a few words at a venture.

Betwixt every other two cells, at the end of the partition which divides them, a hollow shaft or tunnel is left in the brick-work of the exterior wall; which tunnel, if there be several stories to the building, is carried up through all of them.

Into this tunnel is inserted, under each cell, the bottom of an EARTHEN PIPE (like those applied in England to the tops of chimneys) glazed in the inside. The upper end, opening into the cell, is covered by a seat of cast-iron, bedded into the brick-work; with an aperture, which neither by its size nor shape shall be capable of admitting the body of a man. To gain the tunnel from the inside of the cell, the position of this pipe will of course be slanting. At the bottom of the tunnel, on the outside of the building, an arched opening, so low as scarcely to be discernible, admits of the filth being carried away. No one, who has been at all attentive to the history of prisons, but must have observed how often escapes have been effected or attempted through this channel.

A slight screen, which the prisoner might occasionally interpose, may perhaps not be thought superfluous. This, while it answers the purpose of decency, might be so adjusted as to prevent his concealing from the eye of the inspector any forbidden enterprise.

For each cell, the whole apparatus would not come to many shillings: a small consideration for a great degree of security. In this manner, without any relaxation of the discipline, the advantages of cleanliness, and its concomitant health, may be attained to as great a degree as in most private houses.

It would be regarded, perhaps, as a luxury too great for an establishment of this kind, were I to venture to propose the addition of a WATER-PIPE all around, with a cock to it in each cell. The clear expense would, however, not be quite so great as it might seem: since by this means a considerable quantity of attendance would be saved. To each prisoner, some allowance of water must necessarily be afforded, if it were only to drink, without regard to cleanliness. To forward that allowance by hand to two or three hundred prisoners in so many different apartments, might perhaps be as much as one man could do, if constantly employed. For the raising the water by pumps to necessary elevation, the labour of the prisoners would suffice.

As to the MATERIALS, brick, as every body knows, would be the cheapest in ***, and either brick or stone, in every other part of England. Thus much as to the shell. But in a building calculated for duration, as this would be, the expense of allowing the same materials to the FLOORS, and laying them upon ARCHES, would, I imagine, not be deemed an unsuitable one; especially when the advantage of a perfect security from fire is taken into account.

As to the *cells*, they will of course be more or less spacious, according to the employment which it is designed should be carried on in them.

As to the *whole building*, if it be too small, the circumference will not be large enough to afford a sufficient number of cells: if too large, the depth from the exterior windows will be too great; and there will not be light enough in the lodge.

As to this individual building of my brother's, the dimensions of it were determined by the consideration of the most convenient scantlings of the timbers, (that being in his situation the cheapest material), and by other local considerations. It is to have two stories, and the diameter of the whole building is to be 100 feet out and out.

Merely to help conception, I will take this size for an example of such a building as he would propose for England.

Taking the diameter 100 feet, this admits of 48 *cells*, 6 feet wide each at the outside, walls included; with a *passage* through the building, of 8 or 9 feet.

I begin with supposing two stories of cells.

In the *under* story, thickness of the walls 2½ feet.

From thence, clear *depth* of each cell from the window to the grating, 13 feet.

From thence to the ends of the *partition walls*, 3 feet more; which gives the length of the *protracted partitions*.

Breadth of the *intermediate area*, 14.

Total from the outside of the building to the *lodge*, 32½ feet.

The double of this, 65 feet, leaves for the *diameter of the lodge*, 35 feet; including the thickness of its walls.

In the *upper* story, the *cells* will be but 9 feet deep; the difference between that and the 13 feet, which is their depth in the under story, being taken up by a *gallery* which surrounds the protracted partitions.

This gallery supplies, in the upper story, the place of an intermediate area on that floor; and by means of *steps*, which I shall come to presently, forms the communication between the upper story of cells to which it is attached, and the lower story of the cells, together with the intermediate area and the lodge.

The spot most remote from the place where the light comes in from, I mean the *centrical* spot of the building and of the lodge, will not be more than 50 feet distant from that place;

a distance not greater, I imagine, than what is often times exemplified in churches; even in such as are not furnished in the manner of this building, with windows in every part of the exterior boundary. But the inspector's *windows* will not be more than about 32½ feet from the open light.

It would be found convenient, I believe, on many accounts, and in most instances, to make *one story of the lodge* serve for *two stories* of the *cells*; especially in any situation where ground is valuable, the number of persons to be inspected large, the room necessary for each person not very considerable, and frugality and necessity more attended to than appearance.

For this purpose, the *floor* of the *ground story of the lodge* is elevated to within about 4½ feet of the floor of the *first story* of the *cells*. By this means, the inspector's eye, when he stands up, will be on, or a little above, the level of the floor of the above mentioned upper story of the cells; and, at any rate, he will command both that and the ground story of the cells without difficulty, and without change of posture.

As to the *intermediate area*, the *floor* of it is upon a level, not with the *floor* of the *lodge*, but with that of the *lower story* of the cells. But at the *upper* story of the cells, its place, as I have already mentioned, is supplied by the above-mentioned *gallery;* so that the altitude of this area from the floor to the ceiling is equal to that of both stories of the cells put together.

The floor of the lodge not being on a level with either story of the cells, but between both, it must at convenient intervals be provided with flights of *steps*, to go *down* to the ground story of the cells by the intermediate area, and *up* to the first floor of the cells by the gallery. The ascending flights, joined to the *descending*, enable the servants of the house to go to the upper story of the cells, without passing through the apartment of the inspector.

As to the *height* of the whole, and of the several parts, it is supposed that 18 feet might serve for *the two stories of cells*, to be inspected, as above, by *one story* of the *lodge*. This would hold 96 persons.

36 feet for four stories of *cells*, and two of the lodge: this would hold 192 persons.

54 feet for six stories of the cells, and three of the lodge: this would hold 288 persons.

And 54 feet, it is conceived, would not be an immoderate elevation.

The drawings which, I believe, will accompany this, suppose *four* for the number of stories of the cells.

You will see, under the head of hospitals, the reasons why I conceive that even a less height than 9 feet, deducting the thickness of a floor supported by arches, might be sufficient for the cells.

The *passage* might have, for its *height*, either the height of one story, or of two stories of the cells, according as the number of those cells was two or four. The part over the passage might, in either case, be added to the lodge, to which it would thereby give a communication, at each end, with the world without doors, and ensure a keeper against the danger of finding himself a prisoner among his prisoners.

Should it be thought, that, in this way, the lodge would not have light enough, for the convenience of a man of a station competent to the office, the deficiency might be supplied by a void space left in that part, all the way up. You may call it if you please the *central area*. Into this space windows may open where they are wanted, from the apartments of the lodge. It may be either left *open* at the top, or covered with a *sky-light*. But this expedient, though it might add, in some respects, to the convenience of the lodge, could not but add considerably to the quantity and expense of the building.

On the other hand, it would be assistant to ventilation. Here, too, would be a proper place for the *chapel:* the prisoners remaining in their cells, and the windows of the lodge, which is almost all window, being thrown open. The advantages derivable from it in point of light and ventilation depending upon its being kept vacant, it can never be wanted for any profane use. It may therefore, with the great propriety, be allotted to divine service, and receive a regular consecration. The *pulpit* and *sounding-board* may be moveable. During the term of service, the sky-light, at all other times kept as open as possible, might be shut.

LETTER IV.
THE PRINCIPLE EXTENDED TO UNCOVERED AREAS.

IN my two last letters, I gave you such idea as it was in my power to give you by words, of this new plan of construction, considered in its most *simple* form. A few more with regard to what further *extensions* it may admit of.

The utmost number of persons that could be stowed in a single building of this sort, consistently with the purposes of each several institution, being ascertained, to increase the number, that of the buildings must of course be increased. Suppose *two* of these *rotundas* requisite: these two might, *by a covered gallery* constructed upon the same principles, be consolidated into one inspection-house. And by the help of such a covered gallery, *the field of inspection* might be dilated to any extent.

If the number of rotundas were extended to *four*, a regular uncovered area might in that way be inclosed; and being surrounded by covered galleries, would be commanded in this manner from all sides, instead of being commanded only from one.

The area thus inclosed might be either *circular* like the buildings, or *square*, or *oblong*, as one or other of those forms were best adapted to the prevailing ideas of beauty or local convenience. A chain of any length, composed of inspection-houses adapted to the same or different purposes, might in this way be carried round an area of any extent.

On such a plan, either one inspector might serve for two or more rotundas, or if there were one to each, *the inspective force*, if I may use the expression, would be greater in such a compound building, than in any of the number singly taken, of which it was composed; since each inspector might be relieved occasionally by every other.

In the uncovered area thus brought within the field of inspection, out-door employments, or any employments requiring a greater covered space than the general form of construction will allow, might be carried on upon the same principle. A kitchen-garden might then be cultivated for the use of the whole society, by a few members of it at a time, to whom such an opportunity of airing and exercising themselves would be a refreshment and indulgence.

Many writers have expatiated with great force and justice, on the unpopular and unedifying cast of that undistinguishing discipline, which, in situation and treatment, confounds the lot of those who *may* prove innocent, with the lot of those who *have been* proved to be guilty. The same roof, it has been said, ought not to inclose persons who stand in predicaments so dissimilar. In a combination of inspection-houses, this delicacy might be observed without any abatement of that vigilance with regard to safe custody, which in both cases is equally indispensable.

LETTER V.
ESSENTIAL POINTS OF THE PLAN.

IT may be of use, that among all the particulars you have seen, it should be clearly understood what circumstances are, and what are not, essential to the plan. The essence of it consists, then, in the *centrality* of the inspector's situation, combined with the well-known and most effectual contrivances for *seeing without being seen*. As to the *general form* of the building, the most commodious for most purposes seems to be the circular: but this is not an absolutely essential circumstance. Of all figures, however, this, you will observe, is the only one that affords a perfect view, and the same view, of an indefinite number of apartments of the same dimensions: that affords a spot from which, without any change of situation, a man may survey, in the same perfection, the whole number, and without so much as a change of posture, the half of the whole number, at the same time: that, within a boundary of a given extent, contains the greatest quantity of room: – that places the centre at the least distance from the light: – that gives the cells most width, at the part where, on account of the light, most light may, for the purposes of work, be wanted: – and that reduces to the greatest possible shortness the path taken by the inspector, in passing from each part of the field of inspection to every other.

You will please to observe, that though perhaps it is the most important point, that the persons to be inspected should always feel themselves as if under inspection, at least as standing a great chance of being so, yet it is not by any means the *only* one. If it were, the same advantage might be given to buildings of almost any form. What is also of importance is, that for the greatest proportion of time possible, each man should actually *be* under inspection. This is material in *all* cases, that the inspector may have the satisfaction of knowing, that the discipline actually has the effect which it is designed to have: and it is more particularly material in such cases where the inspector, besides seeing that they conform to such standing rules as are prescribed, has more or less frequent occasion to give them such transient and incidental directions as will require to be given and enforced, at the commencement at least of every course of industry. And I think, it needs not much argument to prove, that the business of inspection, like every other, will be performed to a greater degree of perfection, the less trouble the performance of it requires.

Not only so, but the greater chance there is, of a given person's being at a given time actually under inspection, the more strong will be the persuasion – the more *intense*, if I may say so, the *feeling*, he has of his being so. How little turn soever the greater number of persons so circumstanced may be supposed to have for calculation, some rough sort of calculation can scarcely, under such circumstances, avoid forcing itself upon the rudest mind. Experiment, venturing first upon slight trangressions, and so on, in proportion to success, upon more and more considerable ones, will not fail to teach him the difference between a loose inspection and a strict one.

It is for these reasons, that I cannot help looking upon every form as less and less eligible, in proportion as it deviates from the *circular*.

A very material point is, that room be allotted to the lodge, sufficient to adapt it to the purpose of a complete and constant habitation for the principal inspector or head-keeper, and his family. The more numerous also the family, the better; since, by this means, there will in fact be as many inspectors, as the family consists of persons, though only one be paid for it. Neither the orders of the inspector himself, nor any interest which they may feel, or not feel, in the regular performance of his duty, would be requisite to find them motives adequate to the purpose. Secluded oftentimes, by their situation, from every other object, they will naturally, and in a manner unavoidably, give their eyes a direction conformable to that purpose, in every momentary interval of their ordinary occupations. It will supply in their instance the place of that great and constant fund of entertainment to the sedentary and vacant in towns – the looking out of the window. The scene, though a confined, would be a very various, and therefore, perhaps, not altogether an unamusing one.

LETTER VI.
ADVANTAGES OF THE PLAN.

I FLATTER myself there can now be little doubt of the plan's possessing the fundamental advantages I have been attributing to it: I mean, the *apparent omnipresence* of the inspector (if divines will allow me the expression,) combined with the extreme facility of his *real presence*.

A collateral advantage it possesses, and on the score of frugality a very material one, is that which respects the *number* of the inspectors requisite. If this plan required more than another, the additional number would form an objection, which, were the difference to a certain degree considerable, might rise so high as to be conclusive: so far from it, that a greater multitude than ever were yet lodged in one house might be inspected by a single person; for the trouble of inspection is diminished in no less proportion than the strictness of inspection is increased.

Another very important advantage, whatever purposes the plan may be applied to, particularly where it is applied to the severest and most coercive purposes, is, that the *under* keepers or inspectors, the servants and subordinates of every kind, will be under the same irresistible controul with respect to the *head* keeper or inspector, as the prisoners or other persons to be governed are with respect to *them*. On the common plans, what means, what possibility, has the prisoner of appealing to the humanity of the principal for redress against the neglect or oppression of subordinates in that rigid sphere, but the *few* opportunities which, in a crowded prison, the most conscientious keeper *can* afford – but the none at all which many a keeper *thinks* fit to give them? How different would their lot be upon this plan!

In no instance could his subordinates either perform or depart from their duty, but he must know the time and degree and manner of their doing so. It presents an answer, and that a satisfactory one, to one of the most puzzling of political questions – *quis custodiet ipsos custodes?* And, as the fulfilling of his, as well as their, duty would be rendered so much easier, than it can ever have been hitherto, so might, and so should, any departure from it be punished with the more inflexible severity. It is this circumstance that renders the influence of this plan not less beneficial to what is called *liberty*, than to necessary coercion; not less powerful as a controul upon subordinate power, than as a curb to delinquency; as a shield to innocence, than as a scourge to guilt.

Another advantage, still operating to the same ends, is the great load of trouble and disgust which it takes off the shoulders of those occasional inspectors of a higher order, such as *judges* and other *magistrates*, who, called down to this irksome task from the superior ranks of life, cannot but feel a proportionable repugnance to the discharge of it. Think how it is with them upon the present plans, and how it still must be upon the best plans that have been hitherto devised! The cells or apartments, however constructed, must, if there be nine hundred of them (as there were to have been upon the penitentiary-house plan,) be opened to the visitors, one by one. To do their business to any purpose, they must approach near to, and come almost in contact with each inhabitant; whose situation being watched over according to no other than the loose methods of inspection at present practicable, will on that account require the more minute and troublesome investigation on the part of these occasional superintendents. By this new plan, the disgust is entirely removed, and the trouble of going into such a room as the lodge, is no more than the trouble of going into any other.

Were *Newgate* upon this plan, all Newgate might be inspected by a quarter of an hour's visit to Mr. Akerman.

Among the other causes of that reluctance, none at present so forcible, none so unhappily well grounded, none which affords so natural an excuse, nor so strong a reason against accepting of any excuse, as the danger of *infection* – a circumstance which carries death, in one of its most tremendous forms, from the seat of guilt to the seat of justice, involving in one common catastrophe the violator and the upholder of the laws. But in a spot so constructed, and under a course of discipline so insured, how should infection ever arise? or how should it continue? Against every danger of this kind, what private house of the poor, one might almost say, or even of the most opulent, can be equally secure?

Nor is the disagreeableness of the task of superintendence diminished by this plan, in a much greater degree than the efficacy of it is increased. On all others, be the superintendent's visit ever so unexpected, and his motions ever so quick, time there must always be for preparations blinding the real state of things. Out of nine hundred cells, he can visit but one at a time, and, in the meanwhile, the worst of the others may be arranged, and the inhabitants threatened, and tutored how to receive him. On this plan, no sooner is the superintendent announced, than the whole scene opens instantaneously to his view.

In mentioning inspectors and superintendents who are such by office, I must not overlook that system of inspection, which, however little heeded, will not be the less useful and efficacious: I mean, the part which individuals may be disposed to take in the business, without intending, perhaps, or even without thinking of, any other effects of their visits, than the gratification of their own particular curiosity. What the inspector's or keeper's family are with respect to *him*, that, and more, will these spontaneous visitors be to the superintendent, – assistants, deputies, in so far as he is faithful, witnesses and judges should he ever be unfaithful, to his trust. So as they are but there, what the motives were that drew them thither is perfectly immaterial; whether the relieving of their anxieties by the affecting prospect of their respective friends and relatives thus detained in durance, or merely the satisfying that general curiosity, which an establishment, on various accounts so interesting to human feelings, may naturally be expected to excite.

You see, I take for granted as a matter of course, that under the necessary regulations for preventing interruption and disturbance, the doors of these establishments will be, as, without very special reasons to the contrary, the doors of all

public establishments ought to be, thrown wide open to the
body of the curious at large – the great *open committee* of the
tribunal of the world. And who ever objects to such publicity,
where it is practicable, but those whose motives for objection
afford the strongest reasons for it?

LETTER VII.
PENITENTIARY-HOUSES – SAFE CUSTODY.

DECOMPOSING the plan, I will now take the liberty of offering
a few separate considerations, applicable to the different
purposes to which it appears capable of being applied.

A *Penitentiary-house*, more particularly is (I am sorry I must
correct myself, and say, was to have been) what every prison
might, and in some degree at least ought to be, designed at once
as a place of *safe custody*, and a place of *labour*. Every such place
must necessarily be, whether designed or not, an *hospital* –
a place where sickness will be found at least, whether provision
be or be not made for its relief. I will consider this plan in its
application to these three distinguishable purposes.

Against *escapes*, and in particular on the part of felons of
every description, as well before as after conviction, persons
from the desperateness of whose situation attempts to escape
are more particularly to be apprehended, it would afford, as I
dare say you see already, a degree of security, which, perhaps,
has been scarce hitherto reached by conception, much less by
practice. Overpowering the guard requires an union of hands,
and a concert among minds. But what union, or what concert,
can there be among persons, no one of whom will have set eyes
on any other from the first moment of his entrance? Under-
mining walls, forcing iron bars, requires commonly a concert,
always a length of time exempt from interruption. But who
would think of beginning a work of hours and days, without
any tolerable prospect of making so much as the first motion
towards it unobserved? Such attempts have been seldom made
without the assistance of implements introduced by accom-
plices from without. But who would expose themselves even
to the slightest punishment, or even to the mortification of
the disappointment, without so much as a tolerable chance
of escaping instantaneous detection? – Who would think of

bringing in before the keeper's face, so much as a small file, or a phial of *aqua fortis*, to a person not prepared to receive any such thing, nor in a condition to make use of it?* Upon all plans hitherto pursued, the thickest walls have been found occasionally unavailing: upon this plan, the thinnest would be sufficient – a circumstance which must operate, in a striking degree, towards a diminution of the expense.

In this, as in every other application of the plan, you will find its lenient, not less conspicuous than its coercive, tendency; insomuch that, if you were to be asked who had most cause to wish for its adoption, you might find yourself at some loss to determine between the malefactors themselves, and those for whose sake they are consigned to punishment.

In this view I am sure you cannot overlook the effect which it would have in rendering unnecessary that inexhaustible fund of disproportionate, too often needless, and always unpopular severity, not to say torture – the use of *irons*. Confined in one of these cells, every motion of the limbs, and every muscle of the face exposed to view, what pretence could there be for exposing to this hardship the most boisterous malefactor? Indulged with perfect liberty within the space allotted to him, in what worse way could he vent his rage, than by beating his head against the walls? and who but himself would be a sufferer by such folly? Noise, the only offence by which a man thus engaged could render himself troublesome (an offence, by the bye, against which irons themselves afford no security,) might, if found otherwise incorrigible, be subdued by *gagging* – a most natural and efficacious mode of prevention, as well as punishment, the prospect of which would probably be for ever sufficient to render the infliction of it unnecessary. Punishment, even in its most hideous forms, loses its odious character, when bereft of that *uncertainty*, without which the rashest desperado would not expose himself to its stroke. If an instance be wanted, think

---

* Should such strictness be thought requisite, visitors, if admitted into the intermediate area, might be precluded by a rail, from approaching nearer than to a certain distance from the cells; and, in some cases, all conversation between them and the prisoners might be interdicted altogether. The propriety of such a regulation may be thought to stand upon a different footing, according as the confinement were previous or subsequent to conviction, and according to the nature of the offence, and the intended severity of the punishment.

what the means are, which the so much admired law of England makes use of, and that in one of its most admired branches, to work, not upon criminals, but upon its favourite class of judges? what but death? and that no common death, but death the slow but necessary result of lingering torture. And yet, whatever other reproach the law may be thought to merit, in what instance was it ever seen to expose itself in this way to the reproach of cruelty?

LETTER VIII.
USES – PENITENTIARY-HOUSES
– REFORMATION.

IN my last, I endeavoured to state to you the advantages which a receptacle, upon the plan of the proposed building, seemed to promise in its application to places of *confinement*, considered merely in that view. Give me leave now to consider it as applicable to the joint purposes of *punishment, reformation*, and *pecuniary economy*.

That in regard to persons of the description of those to whom punishments of the nature in question are destined, solitude is in its nature subservient to the purpose of reformation, seems to be as little disputed, as its tendency to operate in addition to the mass of sufferance. But that upon this plan that purpose would be effected, at least as completely as it could be on any other, you cannot but see at the first glance, or rather you must have observed already. In the condition of *our* prisoners (for so I will call them for shortness sake) you may see the student's paradox, *nunquam minus solus quam cum solus*, realized in a new way: to the keeper, a *multitude*, though not a *crowd*; to themselves, they are *solitary* and *sequestered* individuals.

What is more, you will see this purpose answered more completely by this plan, than it could possibly be on any other. What degree of solitude it was proposed to reduce them to in the once-intended penitentiary-houses, need not be considered. But for one purpose, in buildings of any mode of construction that could then and there have been in view, it would have been necessary, according to the express regulations of that plan, that the law of solitude should be dispensed with; I mean, so often as the prisoners were to receive the benefits of attendance on Divine service. But in my brother's circular penitentiary-houses, they might receive these benefits, in every circumstance, without stirring from their cells. No thronging nor jostling in the way between the scene of work and the scene destined to devotion; no quarellings, nor confederatings, nor plottings to escape; nor yet any whips or fetters to prevent it.

LETTER IX.
PENITENTIARY-HOUSES – ECONOMY
– CONTRACT – PLAN.

I AM come now to the article of *pecuniary economy*; and as this is the great rock upon which the original penitentiary-plan I understand has split, I cannot resist the temptation of throwing out a few hints relative to the mode of management, which I look upon as the most eligible in this view; but which could not, as you will see, have been established with anything like the advantage, upon any other ground than that of my brother's inspection principle.

To come to the point at once, I would do the whole by *contract*. I would farm out the profits, the no-profits, or if you please the losses, to him who, being in other respects unexceptionable, offered the best terms. Undertaking an enterprise new in its extent, in the description of the persons to be subjected to his management, and in many other circumstances, his success in it, if he does succeed, may be regarded in the light of an invention, and rewarded accordingly, just as success in other inventions is rewarded, by the profit which a monopoly secured by patent enables a man to make; and that in proportion to the success which constitutes their merit. He should have it during *good behaviour*; which you know is as much as to say, unless specific instances of misbehaviour, flagrant enough to render his removal expedient, be proved on him in a legal way, he shall have it for his *life*. Besides that when thus secured he can afford to give the better price for his bargain, you will presently see more material reasons to counterbalance the seeming unthriftiness of granting him a term, which may prove so long a one. In other respects, the terms of the contract must, of course, depend upon the proportion of capital, of which the contract gave him the use. Supposing the advance to amount to the whole manufacturing stock, he must of course either pay something for his contract, or be contented with a *share* of the gross profits, instead of the whole, unless that from such profits an interest upon the capital so advanced to him should be deducted: in which case, nobody, I suppose, would grudge him the whole net profit after such deduction, even though the rate of interest were much below the ordinary one: the difference between such reduced rate of interest and the ordinary one, would constitute the whole of the expense which the public would be at. Suppose, to speak at random, this expense were to amount to £6000, £8000, or £10,000 a-year, for the 3000 convicts which, it was computed, would be the standing number to be maintained in England,* I should not imagine that such a sum as even this latter would be much grudged. I fancy the intended expedition to Botany Bay, of which I am just apprized, will be rather more expensive. Not that it appears to me that the nation would remain saddled with any such expense as this at the long run, or indeed with any part of it. But of this hereafter.

In the next place, I would give my contractor all the *powers* that his interest could prompt him to wish for, in order to enable him to make the most of his bargain, with only some slight reservations, which I will mention afterwards; for very slight ones you will find they will be, that can be needful or even serviceable in the view of preventing abuse.

But the greater latitude he has in taking such measures, the less will he grudge the letting it be known what the measures are which he *does* take, knowing, at the same time, that no advantage can be taken of such knowledge, by turning him out in case of his success, and putting in another to reap the fruits of his contrivance. I will then require him to *disclose*, and even to print and *publish* his accounts – the whole process and detail of his management – the whole history of the prison. I will require him, I say, on pain of forfeiture or other adequate punishment, to publish these accounts, and that upon oath. I have no fear of his not publishing *some* accounts, because, if

---

* According to the hard-labour bill, 2865. See the table to my View of that bill: since then, I fear, the number has rather increased than diminished.

the time is elapsed and some accounts not published – a fact
not liable to dispute – the punishment takes place of course:
and I have not much fear that the accounts, when published,
will not be *true*; because, having power to do every thing that
is for his advantage, there is nothing which it is his interest
to conceal; and the interest which the punishment for perjury
gives him not to conceal, is manifest, more especially as
I make him examinable and cross-examinable *viva voce* upon
oath at any time.

It is for clearing away as much as possible every motive
of pecuniary interest that could prompt him to throw any kind
of cloak or reserve upon any of his expedients for increasing
his profits, that I would insure them to him for *life*.

From the information thus got from him, I derive this
advantage. In the case of his *ill* success, I see the causes of
it, and not only I, but every body else that pleases, may see
the causes of it; and amongst the rest, those who, in case of
their taking the management out of his hands, would have
an interest in being acquainted with such causes, in order to
obviate or avoid them. More than that, if his ill success is owing
to incapacity, and that incapacity such as, if continued, might
raise my expense above the calculation, I can make him stop
in time – a measure to which he can have as little objection
as myself; for it is one advantage of this plan, that whatever
mischief happens must have more than eaten out all *his*
profits before it reaches *me*.

In the case of his good success, I see the causes of that too;
and every body sees them, as before; and, amongst others, all
persons who could propose to themselves to get into a situation
similar to his, and who in such case would naturally promise
themselves, in the event of their getting into his situation,
a success equal to his – or rather superior; for such is the
presumption and vanity natural to man.

Without such publication, whom should I have to deal with,
besides him? certainly, in comparison, but a very few; not
many more than I may have had at first: the terms, of course,
disadvantageous as at first; for disadvantageous terms at first,
while all is yet in darkness, they certainly must be.

After such publication, whom should I have then? I should have
every body; every body who, by fortune, experience, judgment,

disposition, should conceive himself able, and find himself inclined, to engage in such a business; and each person seeing what advantage had been made, and how, would be willing to make his offer in proportion. What situation more favourable for making the best terms?

These best terms, then, I should make at his death, even for his establishment; but long before that, had I others upon the carpet, I should make similar good terms for all those others. Thus I make his advantage mine, not only after it has ceased to be his, but almost as soon as it commences so to be: I thus get his success in all the rest, by paying for it only in the one; and in that not more than it was necessary to pay for it.

But *contractors*, you will say perhaps, or at least if you don't, there are enough that will, '*are a good-for-nothing set of people; and why should we be fleeced by them? One of them perjured himself not long ago, and we put him into the pillory. They are the same sort of gentry that are called farmers-general in France, and publicans in the Gospel, where they are ranked with sinners; and nobody likes them anywhere.*' All this, to be sure, is very true: but if you put one of them into the *pillory*, you put another of them into the *post-office*; and if in the devoted city five righteous would have screened the whole gang from the perdition called for by the enormities of ninety-five unrighteous, why should not the merits of one Palmer be enough to make it up for the demerits of twenty Atkinsons? Gentlemen in general, as I have had manifold occasion to observe, love close reasoning, and here they have it. It might be thought straying from the point, if I ventured to add, that gentlemen in the corn trade, or in any other trade, have not commonly quite so many witnesses to *their bargains*, as my contractor would have to the management of *his* house.

LETTER X.
CHOICE OF TRADES SHOULD BE FREE.

In my last I troubled you with my sentiments on the duration of the first contract, and the great article of *publicity* in the management, which was my motive for admitting of a duration so unlimited. But long before my contractor and I had come to any settlement about these points, he would have found various questions to propose to me. One thing he would not fail to say to me is – *What trades may I put my men to when I have got them?* My answer is soon given. *Any whatever that you can persuade them to turn their hands to.* Now, then, Sir, let us think for a moment, if you please, what trades it may be most for his *advantage* to put them to, and what it is therefore *most likely* he should be disposed to put them to.

That he may get the better view of them, I throw them into *four* classes. In the *first*, I place those who already are possessed of business capable of being carried on with advantage in the prison: in the *second*, those trained up to businesses which, though not capable in themselves of being carried on within such limits, yet by the similarity of operation have a tendency to render it more or less easy for a man to learn some of those other businesses which *are*: in the *third* rank, I would place such as had been trained up indeed to industry, but to branches which have no such tendency as I have just mentioned; such, for instance, as porters, coal-heavers, gardeners, and husbandmen. In the last I would place men regularly brought up to the profession of thieving, and others who have never been brought up to any kind of industry. Some names for these different classes I may as well endeavour to find as not; for names they must have when they get into their house; and if I perform not that business myself, somebody else must do it for me. I will call them the *good* hands, the *capable* hands, the *promising* hands, and the *drones*. As to the *capable* hands, they will, of course, be the more valuable, the nearer the businesses they understand approach to those of the *good* ones; in other words, the less difficulty there would be in teaching the latter the business of the former. The same observation of course applies to the *promising* hands; in as far as the advantage which the one possess by habit the others may appear to possess by disposition. Lower down in the scale of detail I will not attempt to lead you.

You have a very pretty law in England for enriching the country, by keeping boys backward, and preventing men from following the trades they could get most by. If I were jealous of Russia's growing too rich, and being able to buy too many of our goods, I would try to get such a law as that introduced

among these stupid people here, who have never yet had the
sense to think of any such thing. Having no such jealousy
against any country, much less against my own Utopia,
I would beg that law might be banished from within my walls.
I fancy my contractor would be as well pleased with its room
as its company; and as the same indulgence has been granted
to other persons of whose industry no great jealousy seems to
be entertained, such as soldiers and sailors, I have no great
fear the indulgence would be denied me. Much I believe is not
apprehended in that way from the red-coats and jack-tars; and
still less, I believe, would be apprehended from my heroes.

This stumbling-block cleared away, the first thing I imagine
my contractor would do, would be to set to work his *good*
hands; to whom he would add as many of his *capable* hands as
he could muster.

With his *promising* hands and his *drones*, he would set up
a manufacture. What, then, shall this manufacture be? *It may
be this, and that, and t'other thing*, says the hard-labour bill:
it shall be anything or everything, say I.

As to the question, *What sort of manufacture or manufacturer would be likely to answer best?* it is a discussion I will
not attempt to lead you into, for I do not propose at present
to entertain you with a critical examination of the several
actual and possible manufactures, established and establish-
able in Great Britain. The case, I imagine, would be, that some
manufacturer or other would be the man I should have for my
contractor – a man who, being engaged in some sort of business
that was easy to learn, and doing pretty well with as many
hands as he was able to get upon the ordinary terms, might
hope to do better still with a greater number, whom he could
get upon much better terms. Now, whether there are any such
manufacturers, and how many, is what I cannot so well tell
you, especially at this distance; but, if you think it worth while
to ask Mr. Daily Advertiser, or Mr. St. James' Chronicle, I
fancy it will not be long before you get some answer.

In my *View of the Hard-Labour Bill*, I ventured to throw out
a hint upon the subject of putting the good hands to their own
trades. Whether any and what use was made of that hint,
I cannot recollect; for neither the act which passed afterwards,
nor any chapter of that history, has travelled with me to

Crecheff; nor should I have had a single scrap of paper to refresh my memory on that subject, but for the copy of my own pamphlet which I found on my brother's shelf. The general notion seemed to be, that as the people were to be made to work for their punishment, the works to be given to them should be somewhat which they would not like; and, in that respect, it looks as if the consideration of punishment, with its appendage of reformation, had kept the other of economy a little behind the curtain. But I neither see the great danger nor the great harm of a man's liking his work too well; and how well soever he might have liked it *elsewhere*, I should still less apprehend his liking the thought of having it to do *there*. Supposing no sage regulations made by any body to nail them to this or that sort of work, the work they would naturally fall upon under the hands of a contractor would be that, whatever it might be, by which there was most money to be made; for the more the prisoner-workman got, the more the master could get out of him; so that upon that point I should have little fear of their not agreeing. Nor do I see why labour should be the less *reforming* for being profitable. On the contrary, among working men, especially among working men whom the discipline of the house would so effectually keep from all kinds of mischief, I must confess I know of no test of reformation so plain or so sure as the improved quantity and value of their work.

It looks, however, as if the authors of the above provision had not quite so much faith in such an arrangement as I must confess I have. For the choice of the trade was not to be left to the governor of the prison, much less to the prisoner-workman, but was given to *superintending committees of justices of the peace*. In choosing among the employments exemplified, and other similar ones (for if I mistake not this restriction of similarity was subjoined) it was indeed recommended to those magistrates to take 'such employments as they should deem most conducive to profit.' But the profit here declared to be in view was, not the profit of the *workman* or his master the *governor*, but I know not what profit 'of the *district*,' the 'convenience' of which (though I know not what convenience there could be, distinct from profit) was another land-mark given them to steer by. If you cast an eye on the trades exemplified (as I believe I must beg you to do presently) you will find some difficulty, I believe, in conceiving that in the choice of them the article of profit could have been the uppermost consideration. Nor was this all; for besides the vesting of the choice of the employments in committees of justices in the first instance, the same magistrates are called upon to exercise their judgment and ingenuity in dividing the prisoners into classes; in such sort, that the longer a man had stayed in the house his labour should be less and less 'severe,' exception made for delinquency, in which case a man might at any time be turned down from an upper class to a lower. But had the matter been left to a contractor and his prisoner-workmen, they would have been pretty sure to pitch upon, and to stick to, what would be most conducive to *their* profit, and by *that* means to the profit of the district; and that without any recommendation. Whether the effect of that recommendation would have been equally sure upon the above-mentioned magistrates, would have remained to be decided by experience. Understanding me to be speaking merely of a magistrate in the abstract, you will forgive my saying, that in this one point I have not quite so great a confidence in a set of gentlemen of that description, as I have in that sort of knave called a contractor. I see no sort of danger, that to the contractor there should be any one object upon earth dearer than the interest of the contractor; but I see some danger that there may be, now and then by accident, some other object rather dearer to the magistrate. Among these rival objects, if we do not always reckon the pleasure of plaguing the contractor, should he and the magistrate chance not to agree, we may however not unfrequently reckon the exercise of his (the magistrate's) own power, and the display of his own wisdom; the former of which, he may naturally enough conceive, was not given to him for nothing, nor the latter confided in without cause. You must, I think, before now have met with examples of men, that had rather a plan of the public's, or even of an individual's for whom they had a more particular regard, should miscarry under their management, than prosper under a different one.

But if, without troubling yourself about general theories of human nature, you have a mind for a more palpable test of the propriety of this reasoning, you may cut the matter short enough, by making an experiment upon a contractor, and trying whether he will give you as good terms with these clogs about him, as he would without them. Sure I am, that, were I in his place, I should require no small abatement to be made to me, if, instead of choosing the employments for my own men, I was liable at every turn to have them taken out of my hands and put to different employments, by A, B, and C to-day, and by X, Y, and Z to-morrow.

Upon the whole, you will not wonder that I should have my doubts at present, whether the plan was rendered much better for these ingenious but complicated refinements. They seemed mighty fine to me at the time, for when I saw contrivance, I expected success proportionable.

LETTER XI.
MULTIPLICATION OF TRADES IS NOT NECESSARY

SO far as to the *choice* of businesses: As to the new ones, I see no reason why any point should be made of *multiplying* them: a single one, well chosen, may answer the purpose, just as well as ever so many more. I mention this, because though it may be easy to find one species of manufacture, or five, or ten, that might answer with workmen so cramped, and in a situation so confined, it might not be quite so easy to find fifty or a hundred. The number of hands for which employment is to be found, can scarcely be admitted as a reason for multiplying the subjects of manufacture. In such a nation as Great Britain, it is difficult to conceive that the greatest number of hands that can be comprised in such an establishment, should be great enough to overstock the market; and if this island of ours is not big enough, this globe of ours is still bigger. In many species of manufacture, the work is performed with more and more advantage, as every body knows, the more it can be divided; and, in many instances, what sets bounds to that division, is rather the number of hands the master can afford to maintain, than any other circumstance.

When one turns to the hard-labour bill, it looks as if the framers of it had been under some anxiety to find out businesses that they thought might do in their penitentiary-houses, and

to make known the result of their discoveries. It accordingly
proposes for consideration a variety of examples. For such of
the prisoners as were to be worked the hardest: 1. treading
in a wheel; 2. drawing in a capstern for turning a mill or
other machine or engine; 3. beating hemp; 4. rasping logwood;
5. chopping rags; 6. sawing timber; 7. working at forges; 8.
smelting. For those who are to be most favoured: 1. making
ropes; 2. weaving sacks; 3. spinning yarn; 4. knitting nets.

I find some difficulty, however, in conceiving to what use this
instruction was destined, unless it were the edification of that
class of legislators, more frequently quoted for worth than
knowledge – the country gentlemen. To some gentlemen of that
respectable description, it might, for aught I know, be matter
of consolation to see that industry could find so many shapes
to assume, on such a stage. But if it was designed to give a
general view of the purposes to which manual labour may be
applied, it goes not very far, and there are publications enough
that go some hundreds of times farther. If the former of its two
chapters was designed as a specimen of such works of a particularly laborious cast, as are capable of being carried on to the
greatest advantage, or with least advance of capital, or with
the greatest security, against workmen of so refractory a complexion – or if either chapter was destined as a specimen of
employments that required least extent of room – in any of
these cases the specimen seems not a very happy one: – 1*st* and
2*d*, Of the *treading in a wheel*, or *drawing in a capstern for
turning a mill*, nothing can be said in respect of pecuniary
productiveness, till the mill, the machine, or the engine, are
specified; nor anything that can be found to distinguish them
from other employments, except the room and the expense
which such implements seem more particularly to require. 3*d*,
Beating of hemp is a business too proverbial to be unknown
to any body, and in those establishments where it has had
compulsion for its motive, has not hitherto, I believe, proved a
very profitable one; and if I may believe people who are of the
trade, and who have no interest to mislead me, hemp beaten by
hand, though it takes more labour, does not fetch so good a
price, as when beaten at a water-mill. 4*th, Rasping logwood*
is an employment which is said by Mr. Howard, I think, and
others, to be carried on in some work-houses of Holland, and I

believe to some profit. But I know it has been carried on like-wise by the natural *primum mobiles*; witness a wind-mill, which, I remember, a tenant of yours employed in this way; and I can conceive few operations in which those natural powers promise to have greater advantage over the human. 5*th, Chopping rags* is a business that can answer no other purpose than the supply-ing materials for paper-mills, which cannot anywhere be estab-lished without a supply of *running-water* – an element which, I am sure in many, and, I am apt to think, in all paper-mills hitherto established, affords for this operation a *primum mobile* much more advantageous than human labour. In the 6*th,* 7*th,* and 8*th* examples, viz. *sawing timber, working at forges,* and *smelting,* I see nothing to distinguish them very remarkably from three hundred others that might be mentioned, unless it be the great room they all of them occupy, the great and expen-sive establishment which they suppose, or the dangerous weapons which they put into the hands of any workman who may be disposed to turn that property to account. 9*th,* As to *rope making,* which stands at the head of the less laborious class, besides being, as I always understood, remarkably otherwise, it has the particular property of taking up more room than, I believe, any other manufacturing employment that was ever thought of. As to the three last articles of the dozen, viz. *weaving sacks, spinning yarn, and knitting nets.* I know of no particular objections that can be made to them, any more than to three score others. But, without going a stone's throw from the table I am writing upon, I could find more than as many businesses, which pay better in England, than these three last, in other respects exceptionable ones, which are as easy to learn, take up as little room, and require a capital nearly, or quite as moderate, to set up. By coming here, if I have learnt nothing else, I have learnt what the human powers are capable of, when unfettered by the arbitrary regulations of an unenlightened age; and gentlemen may say what they please, but they shall never persuade me that in England those powers are in any remarkable degree inferior to what they are in Russia.*

---

* One of my brother's boys, who had not been at nail-making a month, got flogged the other day for making a knife: not that at Crecheff there is any law against ingenuity; but there is against stealing iron and stealing time.

However, not having the mantle of legislation to screen me from the ridicule of going beyond my last, I forbear to specify even what I have under my eye, knowing that in Mr. Arthur Young, a gentleman whom no one can accuse of hiding his candle under a bushel, anybody that chooses it might find an informant, who, on this, as well as so many other important subjects, for every grain of information I could give, could give a thousand.

But without any disparagement to that gentleman, for whose public-spirited labours and well-directed talents no man feels greater respect than I do, there are other persons, who on these same subjects could, for such a purpose, give still more and better information than he, and who would not be less communicative: I mean, as before, Mr. Daily Advertiser and his brethren.

There are two points in politics very hard to compass. One is, to persuade legislators that they do not understand shoemaking better than shoemakers; the other is, to persuade shoemakers that they do not understand legislating better than legislators. The latter point is particularly difficult in our own dear country; but the other is the hardest of all hard things everywhere.

LETTER XII.
CONTRACTOR'S CHECKS.

THE point, then, being settled, what trades the people may be employed in, another question my contractor will ask is, what *powers* he is to have put into his hands, as a means of persuading them to betake themselves to those trades? The shortest way of answering this question will be to tell him what powers he shall *not* have. In the first place then, he shall not starve them. 'What then,' you will say perhaps, 'do you think it likely that he would?' To speak the truth, for my own part I have no great fear of it. But others perhaps might. Besides, my notion is, that the law, in guarding itself against men, ought to do just the contrary of what the judge should do in trying them, especially where there is nothing to be lost by it. The business, you know, of the judge, is to presume them all honest till he is forced to suspect the contrary: the business

of the law is to conclude them all, without exception, to be
the greatest knaves and villains that can be imagined. My
contractor, therefore, I make myself sure, would starve them
– a good many of them at least – if he were let alone. He would
starve, of course, all whom he could not make pay for their
board, together with something for his trouble. But as I should
get nothing by this economy, and might lose some credit by it,
I have no mind it should take place. Bread, though as bad
as wholesome bread can be, they shall have, then, in plenty:
this and water, and nothing else. This they shall be certain
of having, and, what is of full as much consequence, every
body else that pleases shall be certain of their having it.
My brethren of the would-be-reforming tribe may go and look
at it at the baker's: they may weigh it, if they will, and buy
it, and carry it home, and give it to their children or their pigs.
It shall be dealt out by sound of trumpet, if you please;
and Christian starers may amuse themselves with seeing
bad bread dealt out to felons, as Christian ambassadors are
entertained with the sight of bags of bad money counted out
to Janissaries. The latter wonder I saw: the other I assure you
would give me much more pleasure.

With this saving clause, I deliver them over to the
extortioner, and let him make the most of them. Let him sell
porter at the price of port: and 'humble port' at the price of
'imperial tokay:' his customers might grumble, but I don't
think you would, and I am sure I should not: for it is for that
they were put there. Never fear his being so much his own
enemy, as to stand out for a price which nobody will give.

In the next place I don't know that I should be for allowing
him the power of beating his borders, nor, in short, of punishing them in any shape. Anywhere else, such an exemption
must have been visionary and impracticable. Without either
punishment, or interest given him in the profits of his labour
– an interest which, to get the better of so many adverse
motives, must have been a pretty strong one, how could you
have insured a man's doing a single stroke of work? and, even
with such interest, how could you have insured his not doing
all sorts of mischief? As to mischief, I observed to you, under
the article of safe custody, how easy their keeper might make
himself upon that score: and as to work, I flatter myself you

perceive already, that there need be no great fear of a want of inducements adequate to that purpose.

If, after all, it should be insisted that some power of correction would be absolutely necessary – for instance, in the case of a prisoner's assaulting a keeper or teacher at the time of receiving his food or his instruction (a case which, though never very probable, would be always possible) – such a power, though less necessary here than anywhere else, might, on the other hand, be given with less danger. What tyranny could subsist under such a perfect facility of complaint as is the result of so perfect a facility of inspection? But on this head a word is sufficient, after what I have said in considering the general heads of advantage dependent on this principle. Other checks assistant to this are obvious enough. A *correction-book* might be kept, in which every instance of chastisement, with the cause for which it was administered, might be entered upon record: any the slightest act of punishment not entered to be considered as a lawless injury. If these checks be not enough, the presence of one or more persons, besides him by whom the correction was actually administered, might be required as witnesses of the mode and quantum of correction, and of the alleged cause.

But, besides preventing his starving them or using them ill, there is another thing I should be much inclined to do, in order to make it his interest to take care of them. I would make him pay so much for every one that died, without troubling myself whether any care of his could have kept the man alive. To be sure, he would make me pay for this in the contract; but as I should receive it from him afterwards, what it cost me in the long run would be no great matter. He would get underwriter's profit by me; but let him get that, and welcome.

Suppose three hundred prisoners; and that, out of that number of persons of their ages, ten, that is, one out of thirty, ought to die every year, were they taken at large. But the persons of their character and in their condition, it may be expected, will die faster than honest men. Say, therefore, one in twenty, though I believe, as jails stand at present, if no more than one in ten die, or, for aught I know, out of a much smaller number, it may be thought very well. Give the contractor, then, for every man that ought to die, for instance ten pounds: that sum, repeated for every man in twenty among three hundred, will amount to a hundred and fifty pounds. Upon these terms, then, at the end of the year make him pay ten pounds for every man that has actually died within that time; to which you may add, *or escaped*, and I dare say he will have no objection. If by nursing them and making much of them he should find himself at the end of the year a few pounds the richer by his tenderness, who would grudge it him? If you have still any doubt of him, instead of the ten pounds you may put twenty: you will not be much the poorer for it. I don't know, upon second thoughts, whether somewhat of this sort has not been put in practice, or at least proposed, for foundlings. Be that as it may, make but my contractor's allowance large enough, and you need not doubt of his fondness of these his adopted children; of whom whosoever may chance while under his wing to depart this vale of tears, will be sure to leave one sincere mourner at least, without the parade of mourning.

Some perhaps may be for observing, that, upon my own principles, this contrivance would be of no use but to save the useless, since the contractor, of himself, knows better things than not to take care of a cow that will give milk. But, with their leave, I do not mean that even the useless should be starved; for if the judges had thought this proper, they would have said so.

The patrons of the hard-labour bill, proceeding with that caution and tenderness that pervades their whole system, have denied their *governor*, as they call him, the power of whipping. Some penal power, however, for putting a stop to mischief, was, under their plan, absolutely necessary. They preferred, as the mildest and less dangerous power, that of confining a man in a *dark dungeon under ground*, under a bread-and-water diet. I did then take the liberty to object against the choosing, by way of punishment, the putting of a man into a place which differed not from other places in any essential particular, but that of the chance it stood of proving unwholesome; proposing, at the same time, a very simple expedient, by which their ordinary habitations might be made to receive every other property of a dungeon; in short, the making of them dark.

But in one of my brother's inspection-houses, there the man is in his dungeon already (the only sort of dungeon, at least, which I conceive any man need be in,) very safe and quiet. He is likewise entertaining himself with his bread and water, with only one little circumstance in his favour, that whenever he is tired of that regimen, it is in his own power to put himself under a better: unless my contractor chooses to fine himself for the purpose of punishing his boarder – an act of cruelty which I am in no great dread of.

In short, bating the checks you have seen, and which certainly are not very complicated, the plan of establishment which such a principle of construction seems, now at least, if not for the first time, to render eligible, and which as such I have been venturing to recommend, is exactly upon a par, in point of simplicity, with the forced and temporary expedient of the *ballast-lighters* – a plan that has the most perfect simplicity to recommend it, and, I believe, not much else. The chief differences are, that convicts are not, in the inspection-houses, as in those lighters, jammed together in fetters under a master subject to no inspection, and scarce under any controul, having no interest in their welfare or their work, in a place of *secret* confinement, favourable to infection and to escapes.

LETTER XIII.
MEANS OF EXTRACTING LABOUR.

UNDERSTANDING thus much of his situation, my contractor, I conceive, notwithstanding the checks you have seen, will hardly think it necessary to ask me how he is to manage to persuade his boarders to set to work. – Having them under this regimen, what better security he can wish for of their working, and that to their utmost, I can hardly imagine. At any rate, he has much better security than he can have for the industry and diligence of any ordinary journeyman at large, who is paid by the day, and not by the piece. If a man won't work, nothing has he to do, from morning to night, but to eat his bad bread and drink his water, without a soul to speak to. If he will work, his time is occupied, and he has his meat and his beer, or whatever else his earnings may afford him, and not a stroke does he strike

but he gets something, which he would not have got otherwise.
This encouragement is necessary to his doing his utmost: but
more than this is not necessary. It is necessary every exertion
he makes should be sure of its reward; but it is not necessary
that such reward be so great, or any thing near so great, as
he might have had, had he worked elsewhere. The confinement, which is his punishment, preventing his carrying the
work to another market, subjects him to a monopoly; which
the contractor, his master, like any other monopolist, makes,
of course, as much of as he can. The workman lives in a poor
country, where wages are low; but in a poor country, a man
who is paid according to his work will exert himself at least as
much as in a rich one. According to Mr. Arthur Young, and the
very cogent evidence he gives, he should work more: for more
work that intelligent traveller finds always done in dear years
than in plentiful ones: the earnings of one day affording, in the
latter case, a fund for the extravagance of the next. But this is
not all. His master may fleece him, if he pleases, at both ends.
After sharing in his profits, he may again take a profit upon his
expense. He would probably choose to employ both expedients
together. The tax upon earnings, if it stood alone, might possibly appear liable to be evaded in some degree, and be frus-
trated in some cases, by a confederacy between the workmen
and their employers out of doors; the tax upon expenditure, by
their frugality, supposing that virtue to take root in such a soil;
or in some instances, perhaps, by their generosity to their
friends without doors. The tax upon earnings would probably
not be laid on in an open way, upon any other than the *good*
hands; whose traffic must be carried on, with or without his
intervention, between them and their out-of-door employers.
In the trades which he thought proper to set up of himself for
his *capable* hands, his *promising* hands, and his *drones*, the tax
might be levied in a more covert way by the lowering of the
price paid by him, in comparison of the free prices given out of
doors for similar work. Where he is sure of his men, as well
with regard to their disposition to spend as with regard to their
inability to collude, the tax upon expenditure, without any tax
upon profits open or covert, would be the least discouraging: it
would be the least discouraging for the present, as the earnings
would sound greater to their ears; and with a view to the

future, as they would thereby see (I mean such of them as had any hopes of releasement) what their earnings might at that happy period be expected to amount to, in reality as well as in name.

LETTER XIV.
PROVISION FOR LIBERATED PERSONS.

THE circumstance touched upon at the close of my last letter, suggests another advantage, and that not an inconsiderable one, which you will find more particularly, if not exclusively, connected with the contract plan.

The turning of the prisoners' labour into the most profitable channels being left free, depending upon the joint choice of the two only parties interested in pushing the advantage to the utmost, would afford a resource, and that I should conceive a sure one, for the subsistence of the prisoners, after the expiration of their terms. No trade that could be carried on in this state of thraldom, but could be carried on with at least equal advantage in a state of liberty. Both parties would probably find their account in continuing their manufacturing connexion, after the dissolution of every other. The workman, after the stigma cast on him by the place of his abode, would probably not find it so easy to get employment elsewhere. If he got it at all, it would be upon terms proportioned in some measure to the risk which an employer at large might think he would run on his own part, and in some cases to the danger of driving away fellow-workmen, by the introduction of an associate who might prove more or less unwelcome. He would therefore probably come cheaper to his former master than another man would; at the same time that he would get more from him in his free state than he had been used to get when confined.

Whether this resource was in contemplation with the planners of the hard–labour bill, I cannot pretend to say: I find not upon the face of that bill any proof of the affirmative. It provides a sum for each prisoner, partly for present subsistence, partly as a sort of little capital to be put into his pocket upon his discharge. But the sole measure assigned to this sum is the good behaviour of the party, not the sum required to set him up in whatever might have been his trade. Nor had the choice of his employment been left to the governor of the house, still less to the prisoner, but to committees of justices, as I observed before.

As to the Woolwich Academy, all ideas of reformation under that name, and of a continuance of the like industry as a means of future provision, seem there to have been equally out of the question. That they should hire lighters of their own to heave ballast from, does not appear to have been expected; and if any of them had had the fortune to possess trades of their own before, the scraping of gravel for three, five, or seven years together out of the river, had no particular tendency, that I can see, to rub up the recollection of those trades. The allowance upon discharge would, however, always have its use, though not always the same use. It might help to fit them out for trades; it might serve them to get drunk with; it might serve them to buy any house-breaking implements which they could not so well come at to steal. – The separation between the landlord and his guests must on his side have been rendered the less affecting, by the expectation which he could not but entertain of its proving but a short one. Nor was subsequent provision of one sort or other by any means wanting, for those who failed to find it *there*. The gallows was always ready with open arms to receive as many as the jail-fever should have refused.

LETTER XV.
PROSPECT OF SAVING FROM THIS PLAN.

MANY are the data with which a man ought to be furnished (and with not one of which am I furnished) before he pretended to speak upon any tolerable footing of assurance with regard to the advantage that might be expected in the view of pecuniary economy from the inspection plan. *On the one hand*, the average annual amount of the *present* establishments, whatever they are (for I confess I do not know,) for the disposal of convicts: The expected amount of the like average with regard to the measure which I have just learnt has been resolved upon, for sending colonies of them to New South Wales, including as well the maintenance of them till shipped, as the expense of the transportation, and the maintenance of them when they are got there: – *On the other hand*, the capital proposed to have been expended in the *building* and *fitting up* the experimental *penitentiary-house:* —— The further capital proposed to have been expended in the *furniture* of it: – The sum proposed to have been allowed per man for the *maintenance* of the prisoners till the time when their labour might be expected to yield a produce. These points and a few others being ascertained, I should then be curious to know what degree of productiveness, if any would be looked upon as giving to the measure of a penitentiary-house, either of any construction or of this extraordinary one, the pre-eminence upon the whole over any of the other modes of disposal now in practice or in contemplation. Many distinct points for the eye to rest upon in such a scale will readily occur: – 1*st*, The produce might be barely sufficient to pay the expense of *feeding*; – 2*d*, It might farther pay the expense of *clothing*; – 3*d*, It might farther pay the expense of *guarding* and *instructing*, viz. the salaries or other emoluments of the numerous tribe of visitors, governors, jailors, task-masters, &c. in the one case, and of the contractor and his assistants in the other; – 4*th*, It might farther pay the *wear and tear* of the working-stock laid in; – 5*th*, It might farther pay the *interest* of the *capital* employed in the purchase of such stock; – 6*th*, It might farther pay the interest of the capital laid out in the *erecting* and *fitting* up the establishment in all its parts, at the common rate of interest for money laid out in building; – 7*th*, It might farther pay, at the ordinary rate, the *interest* of the money, if any, laid out in the *purchase* of the *ground*. Even at the first mentioned and lowest of these stages, I should be curious to compare the charge of such an institution with that of the least chargeable of those others that are as yet preferred to it. When it had arisen above the last, then, as you see, and not till then, it could be said to yield a profit, in the sense in which the same thing could be said of any manufacturing establishment of a private nature.

But long before that period, the objections of those whose sentiments are the least favourable to such an establishment would, I take for granted, have been perfectly removed. Yet

what should make it stop anywhere short of the highest
of those stages, or what should prevent it from rising even
considerably above the highest of them, is more, I protest, than
I can perceive. In what points a manufacturer setting up in
such an establishment would be in a *worse* situation than an
ordinary manufacturer, I really do not see; but I see many
points in which he is in a *better*. His hands, indeed, are all raw,
perhaps, at least with relation to the particular species of work
which he employs them upon, if not with relation to every
other. But so are all hands everywhere, at the first setting up
of every manufacture. Look round, and you will find instances
enough of manufactures where children, down to four years
old, earn something, and where children a few years older earn
a subsistence, and that a comfortable one. I must leave to you
to mention names and places. You, who have been so much of
an English traveller, cannot but have met with instances in
plenty, if you have happened to note then down. Many are the
instances you must have found in which the part taken by each
workman is reduced to some one single operation of such
perfect simplicity, that one might defy the awkwardest and
most helpless idler that ever existed to avoid succeeding in it.
Among the eighteen or twenty operations into which the
process of pin-making has been divided, I question whether
there is any one that is not reduced to such a state. In this
point, then, he is upon at least as good a footing as other
manufacturers: but in all other points he is upon a better.
What hold can any other manufacturer have upon his workmen, equal to what my manufacturer would have upon his?
What other master is there that can reduce his workmen, if
idle, to a situation next to starving, without suffering them to
go elsewhere? What other master is there, whose men can
never get drunk unless he chooses they should do so? and who,
so far from being able to raise their wages by combination, are
obliged to take whatever pittance he thinks it most for his
interest to allow? In all other manufactories, those members or
a family who can and will work, must earn enough to maintain
not only themselves but those who either cannot or will not
work. Each master of a family must earn enough to maintain,
or at least help to maintain a wife, and to maintain such as are
yet helpless among his children. My manufacturer's workmen,

however cramped in other respects, have the good or ill fortune to be freed from this incumbrance – a freedom, the advantage of which will be no secret to their master, who, seeing he is to have the honour of their custom in his capacity of shopkeeper, has taken care to get the measure of their earnings to a hair's-breadth. What other manufacturers are there who reap their profits at the risk of other people, and who have the purse of the nation to support them, in case of any blameless misfortune? And to crown the whole by the great advantage which is the peculiar fruit of this new principle, what other master or manufacturer is there, who to appearance constantly, and in reality as much as he thinks proper, has every look and motion of each workman under his eye? Without any of these advantages, we see manufacturers not only keeping their heads above water, but making their fortunes every day. A manufacturer in this situation *may* certainly fail, because so may he in any other. But the probability is, he would *not* fail: because, even without these great advantages, much fewer fail than thrive, or the wealth of the country could not have gone on increasing as it has done, from the reign of Brutus to the present. And if political establishments were to wait till probability were converted into certainty before trial, *Parliament* might as well go to bed at once, and sleep on the same pillow with sister *convocation*.

To speak in sober sadness, I do dearly love, as you well know, in human dealings no less than in divine, to think and say, as far as conscience will allow me, that 'whatever is, is right;' as well concerning those things which are done, as concerning those which have been left undone. The gentlemen who gave themselves so much trouble about the penitentiary-house plan, did extremely well; and, for aught I know, the gentlemen who put it under the table at last, may have done still better. If you have a mind to share with me in this comfortable feeling, turn once more to that discarded favourite, and observe what load of expense, some part then necessary, some perhaps not altogether so, it was to have thrown upon the nation; and, at the same time, what will be still more comfortable to you, how great a proportion of that expense would be struck off, by the new and of course still greater favourite, which I have ventured to introduce to you.

In the first place, there was to have been a vast extent of ground; for it was to have had *rope-walks* and *timber-yards*, and it is well it was not to have had dock-yards. Then, for the sake of healthiness, that ground was to have a command of *running water*: then again, for the convenience of dignified inspectors, that ground and that water were to have been in the *vicinity of the metropolis*. It was to have been on the banks of the Thames – somewhere, I think, about Wandsworth and Battersea; and a site fit for I know not how many of the most luxurious villas that fancy could conceive or Christie describe, was to be buried under it. Seven-and-twenty thousand pounds, I think, was the price talked of, and, for aught I know, paid, for the bare ground, before so much as a spade was put in it.* As to my contractor, eighteen or twenty acres of the most unprofitable land your country or any other contains, any waste land, in short, which the crown has already in its possession, would answer every plea he could put in; and out of that he would crib gardens for his own accommodation, and farm-yards, and I know not what besides. As to *running water*, it is indeed to every purpose a very agreeable circumstance, and, under the ordinary jail regimen, a very desirable, possibly an essential one. But many of the Lords and Commons make shift without it, even at their villas, and almost all of them when not at their villas, without ascribing any want of health they may labour under to the want of running water. As to my contractor's boarders, they must have water, indeed, because everybody must have water; but under the provision I have made for turning the operations of cleanliness into *motions of course*, I should apprehend their condition might still be tolerable, should they have no other running stock of that necessary element than what falls to the share of better men.

When the ground thus dearly wrung from the grasp of luxury came to be covered, think what another source of expense was to be opened, when, over and above nine hundred roomy chambers for so many persons to *lie* in, three other different classes of apartments were to be provided, to I know not what number nor extent, for them to *work* in, to *pray* in,

---

* I do not recollect from what source I took this idea of the sum. I now understand it to have been no more than five thousand pounds.

and to *suffer* in! – four operations, the scenes of which are, upon our plan, consolidated into one.

I need not add much to what I have said in a former letter, about the tribe of subordinate establishments, each of them singly an object of no mean expense, which it seems to have been in contemplation to inclose within the fortress: I mean the mills, the forges, the engines, the timber-yards, and the rope-walks. The seal which stamps my contract dispels, as if it were a talisman, this great town in *nubibus*; and two or three plain round houses take its place. Either I am much mistaken, or a sum not much exceeding what was paid or destined for the bare ground of the proposed penitentiary-houses, would build and completely fit up those round houses, besides paying for the ground.

To this account of the *dead* stock is to be added, if I may say it without offence, that of the *live* stock of inspectors, of every rank and denomination: I mean the pyramid of under-keepers, and task-masters, and store-keepers, and governors, and committees of magistrates, which it builds up, all to be paid up and salaried, with allowances rising in proportion to the rise of dignity: the whole to be crowned with a grand triumvirate of superintendents, two of whom were to have been members of parliament, men of high birth and quality, whose toilsome dignity a minister would hardly have affronted by the offer of salaries much inferior to what are to be found annexed to sinecures.

I will not say much of the 'other officers,' without number, which I see, by my *View of the Hard-labour Bill*, were to have been added, and of course must have been added, in such number as the 'committees' of your **** to whom this business was then committed, or at any rate some other good judges should have judged 'necessary.'

Officers and governors, *eo nomine*, my contractor would have none: and any superfluous clerk or over-looker, who might be found lurking in his establishment, he would have much less tenderness for, than your gardener has for the sow-thistles in your garden. The greatest part of *his* science comes to *him* in maxims from his grand-mother; and amongst the foremost of those maxims is that which stigmatizes as an unfrugal practice, the keeping of more cats than will catch mice.

If, under all these circumstances, the penitentiary-houses should have been somewhat of a bugbear, it will be the less to be wondered at, when one considers the magnitude of the scale upon which this complicated experiment was going to be made. I mentioned in round numbers nine hundred as the number of convicts which was going to be provided for; but 888 was the exact number mentioned in the bill. Three eights, 'thus arranged, a terrible show!' But granting this to be the number likely to require provision of some kind or other, it surely does not follow that all that require it must necessarily be provided for in this manner, or in none. If the eight hundred and eighty eight appear so formidable, gentlemen may strike off the hundreds, and try whether the country will be ruined by an establishment inferior to that which an obscure ex-countryman of theirs is going to amuse himself with.

What I have all along been taking for granted is, that it is the mere dread of extravagance that has *driven* your thrifty minister from the penitentiary-house plan – not the love of transportation that has *seduced* him from it. The inferiority of the latter mode of punishment in point of exemplarity and equality – in short, in every point but that of expense, stands, I believe, undisputed. I collected the reasons against it, that were in every body's mouth, and marked them down, with, I think, some additions (as you may or may not remember) in my view of the hard-labour bill, supplement included. I have never happened to hear any objections made to those reasons; nor have I heard of any charms, other than those of antiquity and comparative frugality, that transportation has to recommend it. Supposing, therefore, what I most certainly do not suppose, that my contractor could not keep his people at home at *less* expense than it would take to send them abroad, yet if he could keep them at no *greater* expense, I should presume that even this would be reckoned no small point gained, and that even this very moderate success would be sufficient to put an end to so undesirable a branch of navigation.

Nor does any preference that might be given to the transportation plan, supersede the necessity of this or some other substitute to it, in the many cases to which it cannot be conceived that plan should be extended. Transportation to this desert for seven years – a punishment which under such circumstances is so much like transportation for life – is not, I suppose, to be inflicted for every peccadillo. Vessels will not be sailing every week or fortnight upon this four or five or six months navigation: hardly much oftener, I should suppose, than once a twelvemonth. In the meantime, the convicts must be somewhere: and whether they are likely to be better qualified for colonization by lounging in an ordinary jail, or rotting on board a ballast hulk, or working in an inspection-house, may now, I think, be left for any one to judge.

LETTER XVI.
HOUSES OF CORRECTION.

IN considering my brother's inspection plan as applicable to the purpose of establishments designed to force labour, my principal theme has hitherto been the national establishment of *penitentiary-houses*. My first design, however, was to help to drive the nail I saw a-going: I mean the *house of correction*, which the advertisement informed me was under consideration for your ****. I had little notion, at the outset, of attempting any such up-hill work as the heaving up again that huge stone, the *penitentiary-house*, which the builders at last had refused, and which, after the toiling and straining of so many years, had tumbled to the bottom. But the greater object grew upon me as I wrote; and what I found to say on that subject I grudged the less, as thinking it might, most of it, be more or less applicable to your establishment. How far, and in what particular respects, it may prove so, I have no means of knowing: I trouble you with it at a venture. In my last I proposed, if the nation were poor and fearful, a penitentiary-house upon a very small scale – so small, if such caution were thought necessary, as not to contain so many as a hundred prisoners. But however poor the nation may be, the ***** of **** surely is rich. What then should hinder your ***** from standing forth and setting the nation an example? What the number of persons you may have to provide for in this way is supposed to be, I have no means of knowing; but I should think it strange if it did not considerably exceed the one just mentioned. What it is you will risk by such an experiment, is more than I can see. As far as the building is concerned, it is a question which architects, and they alone, can answer. In the meantime, we who know nothing of the matter, can find no reason, all things considered, why a building upon this plan should cost more than upon another. But setting aside the building, every other difference is on the profitable side.

The precautions against escapes, and the restraints destined to answer the ends of punishment, would not, I suppose, in your establishment be quite so strict, as it would be necessary they should be in an establishment designed to answer the purpose of a penitentiary-house. Bars, bolts, and gratings, would in this of your's, I suppose, be rejected; and the inexorable *partition walls* might for some purposes be thinned away to boards or canvass, and for others thrown out altogether. With you, the gloomy paradox of crowded solitude might be exchanged, perhaps, for the cheerfulness of a common refectory. The Sabbath might be a Sabbath there as elsewhere. In the penitentiary inspection-house, the prisoners were to lie, as they were to eat, to work, to pray, and to do every thing, in their cells, and nowhere else. In your house of correction, where they should lie, or how they should lie, I stay not to inquire.

It is well, however, for you **** gentlemen, that you are so rich; for in point of frugality, I could not venture to promise you anything like the success that I would to 'poor old England.' Your contractor's jailbirds, if you had a contractor, would be perpetually upon the wing: the short terms you would be sending them to him for, would seldom admit of their attaining to such a proficiency, as to make a profit upon any branch of industry. In general, what in a former letter I termed the *good* hands, would be his chief, if not his whole dependence; and that, I doubt, but a scanty one.

I will not pester you with further niceties applicable to the difference between *houses of correction*, and *work-houses*, and *poor-houses*, if any there should be, which are not work-houses; between the different modes of treatment that may be due to what are looked upon as the inferior degrees of *dishonesty*, to *idleness* as yet untainted with dishonesty, and to blameless *indigence*. The law herself has scarcely eyes for these microscopic differences. I bow down, therefore, for the present at

least, to the counsel of so many sages, and shrink from the
crime of being 'wiser than the law.'

LETTER XVII.
PRISONS FOR SAFE CUSTODY MERELY.

A WORD or two respecting the condition of *offenders before
conviction*: or, if that expression should appear to include a
solecism, of persons accused, who either for want of bail, or as
charged with offences not bailable, have hitherto been made,
through negligence or necessity, to share by anticipation so
much of the fate of convicts, as imprisonment more or less
rigid may amount to.

To persons thus circumstanced, the inspection principle
would apply, as far as *safe custody* was concerned, with as much
advantage as to convicts. But as there can be no ground for
punishing them any otherwise than in so far as the *restraint*
necessary for safe custody has the effect of punishment, there
can be as little ground for subjecting them to *solitude*; unless
where that circumstance should also appear necessary, either
to safe custody, or to prevent that mental infection, which
novices in the arts of dishonesty, and in debauchery, the parent
of dishonesty, are so much in danger of contracting from the
masters of those arts. In this view, therefore, the *partitions*
might appear to some an unnecessary ingredient in the compo-
sition of the building; though I confess, from the consideration
just alleged, they would not appear in that light to me.
Communication must likewise be allowed to the prisoners with
their friends and legal assistants, for the purpose of settling
their affairs, and concerting their defence.

As forced labour is punishment, labour must not here be
forced. For the same reason, and because the privation of such
comforts of any kind as a man's circumstances allow him, is
also punishment, neither should the free admission of such
comforts, as far as is consistent with sobriety, be denied; nor,
if the keeper is permitted to concern himself in any part of the
trade, should he be permitted to make a greater profit than
would be made by other traders.

But amongst persons of such description, and in such a

multitude, there will always be a certain number, nor that
probably an inconsiderable one, who will possess no means of
subsistence whatever of their own. These then will, in so far,
come under a predicament not very dissimilar to that of
convicts in a penitentiary-house. Whatever works they may
be capable of, there is no reason why subsistence should be
given to them, any more that to persons free from suspicion
and at large, but as the price for work, supposing them able
to perform it. But as this ability is a fact, the judgment of
which is a matter of great nicety, too much it may be thought
by far to be entrusted to such hands, if to any, some allowance
must therefore be made them *gratis*, and that at least as good
a one as I recommended for the penitentiary-house. In order
to supply the defects of this allowance, the point then will be, to
provide some sort of work for such, who not having trades
of their own which they can work at, are yet willing to take
work, if they can get it. If to find such work might be difficult,
even in a house of correction, on account of the shortness of
the time which there may be for learning work, for the same
reason it should be still more difficult in a prison appropriated
to safe custody before conviction, at least in cases where, as
it will sometimes happen, the commitment precedes the trial
but a few days. If on the ground of being particularly likely to
have it in his power to provide work, the contracting keeper
of a penitentiary-house should be deemed the fittest person for
the keeping of a *safe-custody house* (for so I would wish to call
it, rather than a prison,) in other respects he might be thought
less fit, rather than more so. In a penitentiary-house, he is
an extortioner by trade: a trade he must wholly learn, every
time he sets his foot in a safe-custody house, on pain of such
punishment as unlicensed extortioners may deserve. But it by
no means follows, because the keeper of a penitentiary-house
has found one, or perhaps half-a-dozen sorts of work, any of
which a person may make himself tolerably master of in the
course of a few months, that he should be in possession of any
that might be performed without learning, or learnt in a few
days. If, therefore, for frugality's sake, or any other convenience, any other establishments were taken to combine with
that of a safe-custody house, a house of correction would seem
better suited to such a purpose, than a penitentiary-house. But

without considering it as matter of necessity to have recourse
to such shifts, the eligibility of which might depend upon local
and other particular considerations, I should hope that employments would not be wanting, and those capable of affording
a moderately good subsistence, for which a man of ordinary
faculties would be as well qualified the first instant, as at
the end of seven years. I could almost venture to mention
examples, but that the reasons so often given stop my pen.

LETTER XVIII.
MANUFACTORIES.

AFTER so much as has been said on the application of our
principle to the business of manufactories, considered as
carried on by forced labour, you will think a very few words
more than sufficient, in the view of applying it to manufactories
carried on upon the ordinary plan of freedom.

The centrality of the presiding person's situation will have its
use at all events; for the purpose of direction and order at least,
if for no other. The concealment of his person will be of use,
in as far as controul may be judged useful. As to partitions,
whether they would be serviceable in the way of preventing
distraction, or disserviceable by impeding communication,
will depend upon the particular nature of the particular manufacture. In some manufactories they will have a further use, by
the convenience they may afford for ranging a greater number
of tools than could otherwise be stowed within the workman's
reach. In nice businesses, such as that of watch-making, where
considerable damage might result from an accidental jog or
a momentary distraction, such partitions, I understand, are
usual.

Whatever be the manufacture, the utility of the principle is
obvious and incontestible, in all cases where the workmen are
paid according to their *time*. Where they are paid by the *piece*,
there the interest which the workman has in the value of his
work supersedes the use of coercion, and of every expedient
calculated to give force to it. In this case, I see no other use to be
made of the inspection principle, than in as far as instruction
may be wanted, or in the view of preventing any waste or

other damage, which would not of itself come home to the
workman, in the way of diminishing his earnings, or in any
other shape.

Were a manufactory of any kind to be established upon this
principle, the *central lodge* would probably be made use of
as the compting-house: and if more branches than one were
carried on under the same roof, the accounts belonging to each
branch would be kept in the corresponding parts of the lodge.
The lodge would also serve as a sort of temporary store-room,
into which the tools and materials would be brought from the
work-houses, and from whence they would be delivered out
to the workmen all around, as well as finished work received,
as occasion might require.

LETTER XIX.
MAD-HOUSES.

I COME now with the pleasure, notwithstanding the sadness of
the subject, to an instance in which the application of the principle will be of the lenient cast altogether: I mean, that of the
melancholy abodes appropriated to the reception of the insane.
And here, perhaps, a noble lord now in administration might
find some little assistance lent to the humane and salutary
regulations for which we are chiefly indebted to his care.*

That any of the receptacles at present subsisting should be
pulled down only to make room for others on the inspection
principle, is neither to be expected nor to be wished. But,
should any buildings that may be erected in future for this
purpose be made to receive the inspection form, the object
of such institutions could scarce fail of receiving some share of
its salutary influence. The powers of the insane, as well
as those of the wicked, are capable of being directed either
against their fellow-creatures or against themselves. If in
the latter case nothing less than perpetual chains should
be availing, yet in all instances where only the former danger
is to be apprehended, separate cells, exposed, as in the case of

---

* Lord Sydney; who in the House of Commons brought in the bill for the regulation of mad-houses, which afterwards passed into an act.

prisons, to inspection, would render the use of chains and other modes of corporal sufferance as unnecessary in this case as in any. And with regard to the conduct of the keepers, and the need which the patients have to be kept, the natural, and not discommendable jealousy of abuse would, in this instance as in the former ones, find a much readier satisfaction than it could anywhere at present.

But without thinking of erecting mad-houses on purpose, if we ask Mr. Howard, he will tell us, if I do not misrecollect, that there are few prisons or work-houses but what are applied occasionally to this use. Indeed, a receptacle of one or other of these descriptions is the ready, and, I believe, the only resource, which magistrates find vested in their hands. Hence it was, he so often found his senses assailed with that strange and unseemly mixture of calamity and guilt – lunatics raving and felons rioting in the same room. But in every penal inspection-house, every vacant cell would afford these afflicted beings an apartment exempt from disturbance, and adapted to their wants.

LETTER XX.
HOSPITALS.

IF any thing could still be wanting to show how far this plan is from any necessary connexion with severe and coercive measures, there cannot be a stronger consideration than that of the advantage with which it applies to *hospitals*; establishments of which the sole object is the relief of the afflicted, whom their own entreaties have introduced. Tenacious as ever of the principle of *omnipresence*, I take it for granted that the whole tribe of medical curators – the *surgeon*, the *apothecary*, the *matron*, to whom I could wish to add even the *physician*, could the establishment be but sufficient to make it worth his while, find in the inspection-lodge and what apartments might be added above it, their constant residence. Here the physician and the apothecary might know with certainty that the prescription which the one had ordered and the other made up, had been administered at the exact time and in the exact manner in which it was ordered to be administered. Here the surgeon would be sure that his instructions and directions had been followed in all points by his pupils and assistants. Here the faculty, in all its branches, might with the least trouble possible watch as much as they chose to watch, of the progress of the disease, and the influence of the remedy. Complaints from the sick might be received the instant the cause of the complaint, real or imaginary, occurred; though, as misconduct would be followed by instant reprehension, such complaints must be proportionably rare.

The separation of the cells might be in part, continued either for comfort, or for decency. Curtains, instead of grating, would give the patients, when they thought fit, the option of being seen. Partitions of greater solidity and extent might divide the fabric into different wards, confining infection, adapting themselves to the varieties of disease, and affording, upon occasion, diversities of temperature.

In hot weather, to save the room from being heated, and the patients from being incommoded by the sun, *shades* or awnings might secure the windows towards the south.

I do not mean to entertain you here with a system of physic, or a treatise upon *airs*. But a word or two on this subject you must permit me. Would the ceilings of the cell be high enough? Is the plan of construction sufficiently favourable to ventilation? I have not the good fortune to have read a book published not long ago on the subject of hospitals, by our countryman Mr. Aikin, though I remember seeing some account of it in a review. But I cannot help begging of you to recommend to the notice of your medical friends, the perusal of Dr. De Maret's paper, in the *Memoirs of the Academy of Dijon* for the year 1782. If either his facts or his reasoning are to be trusted, not only no loftiness of ceiling is sufficient to ensure to such a building a purity of air, but it may appear questionable whether such an effect be upon the whole promoted by that circumstance.*

His great anxiety seems to be, that at some known period or periods of the day, the whole mass of air may undergo at

---

* To an hospital lately built at Lyons, a vast dome had been given in this view. It had been expected that the foul air should be found at top, while that near the floor should have been sweet and wholesome. On the contrary, substances which turned putrid at the bottom in a single day, remained sweet above at the end of five days.

once a total change, not trusting to partial and precarious evacuations by opening here and there a window; still less to any height or other amplitude of room – a circumstance which of itself tends to render them still more partial and precarious. Proscribing all rectilinear walls and flat ceilings forming angles at the junctions, he recommends accordingly for the inside of his building, the form of a long oval, curved in every direction except that of the floor, placing a door at each end. By throwing open these doors, he seems to make it pretty apparent, that the smallest draught will be sufficient to effect an entire change in the whole stock of air; since at which ever end a current of air happens first to enter, it will carry all before it till it gets to the other. Opening windows, or other apertures, disposed in any other part of the room, would tend rather to disturb and counteract the current, than to promote it.

From the same reasoning it will follow, that the *circular* form demanded as the best of all by the inspection principle, must, in a view to ventilation, have in a considerable degree the advantage over *rectilinear*; and even, were the difference sufficiently material, the inspection principle might be applied to his oval with little or no disadvantage. The form of the inspection lodge might in this case follow that of the containing building; and that central part, so far from obstructing the ventilation, would rather, as it should seem, assist it, increasing the force of the current by the compressure.

It should seem also, that to a circular building, the central lodge would thus give the same aptitude to ventilation, which the Doctor's oval form possesses of itself.

To save his patients from catching cold while the current is passing through the room, the Doctor allows to each a short *screen*, like the head of a cradle, to be rested on the bed.

Here the use of the tin *speaking-tubes* would be seen again, in the means they would afford to the patient, though he were equal to no more than a whisper, of conveying to the lodge the most immediate notice of his wants, and receiving answers in a tone equally unproductive of disturbance.

Something I could have wished to say on the important difference between the general and comparatively immaterial impurity resulting merely from the *phlogiston*, and the various particular impurities constituted by the various products of *putrefaction*, or by the different matters of the various *contagions*. Against these very different dangers, the mode and measure of precaution might admit of no small difference. But this belongs not necessarily to the subject, and you would not thank me, any more than gentlemen of the faculty who understand it better than I, or gentlemen at large who would not wish to understand it.

An hospital built and conducted upon a plan of this kind, of the success of which everybody might be an observer, accessible to the patients' friends, who, without incommoding or being incommoded, might see the whole economy of it carried on under their eye, would lose, it is to be hoped, a great part of those repelling terrors, which deprive of the benefit of such institutions many objects whom prejudice, in league with poverty, either debars altogether from relief, or drives to seek it in much less eligible shapes. Who knows but that the certainty of a medical attendance, not occasional, short-lived, or even precarious, as at present, but constant and uninterrupted, might not render such a situation preferable even to home, in the eyes of many persons who could afford to pay for it? and that the erection of a building of this kind might turn to account in the hands of some enterprising practitioner?

A *prison*, as I observed in a former letter, includes an hospital. In prisons on this construction, every cell may receive the properties of an hospital, without undergoing any change. The whole prison would be perhaps a better hospital than any building known hitherto by that name. Yet should it be thought of use, a few cells might be appropriated to that purpose; and perhaps it may be thought advisable that some cases of infection should be thrown out, and lodged under another roof.

But if infection in general must be sent to be *cured* elsewhere, there is no spot in which infection originating in negligence can, either in the *rise* or *spread* of it, meet with such obstacles as here. In what other instance as in this, will you see the interests of the governor and the governed in this important particular, so perfectly confounded and made one? – those of the keeper with those of the prisoners – those of the medical curator with those of the patients? Clean or unclean, safe or unsafe, he runs the chance that they do: if he lets them poison themselves, he lets them poison *him*. Encompassed on all sides by a multitude of persons, whose good or bad condition depends upon himself, he stands as a hostage in his own hands for the salubrity of the whole.

LETTER XXI.
SCHOOLS.

AFTER applying the inspection principle first to prisons, and through mad-houses bringing it down to hospitals, will the parental feeling endure my applying it at last to schools? Will the observation of its efficacy in preventing the irregular application of undue hardship even to the guilty, be sufficient to dispel the apprehension of its tendency to introduce tyranny into the abodes of innocence and youth?

Applied to these, you will find it capable of two very distinguishable degrees of extension: – It may be confined to the hours of study; or it may be made to fill the whole circle of time, including the hours of repose, and refreshment, and recreation.

To the first of these applications the most captious timidity, I think, could hardly fancy an objection: concerning the hours of study, there can, I think, be but one wish, that they should he employed in study. It is scarce necessary to observe that gratings, bars, and bolts, and every circumstance from which an inspection-house can derive a terrific character, have nothing to do here. All play, all chattering – in short, all distraction of every kind, is effectually banished by the central and covered situation of the master, seconded by partitions or screens between the scholars, as slight as you please. The different measures and casts of talent, by this means rendered, perhaps for the first time, distinctly discernible, will indicate the different degrees of attention and modes of culture most suitable to each particular disposition; and incurable and irreproachable dulness or imbecility will no longer be punished for the sins of idleness or obstinacy. That species of fraud at Westminster called *cribbing*, a vice thought hitherto congenial to schools, will never creep in here. That system of premature corruption, in which idleness is screened by opulence, and the

honour due to talents or industry is let out for hire, will be
completely done away; and a nobleman may stand as good a
chance of knowing something as a common man.

Nor, in point of present enjoyment, will the scholars
be losers by the change. Those sinkings of the heart at the
thoughts of a task undone, those galling struggles between
the passion for play and the fear of punishment, would there
be unknown. During the hours of business, habit, no longer
broken in upon by accident, would strip the master's presence
of its terrors, without depriving it of its use. And the time
allotted for study being faithfully and rigidly appropriated to
that service, the less of it would serve.

The separate spaces allotted for this purpose would not in
other respects be thrown away. A bed, a bureau, and a chair,
must be had at any rate; so that the only extraordinary
expense in building would be for the *partitions*, for which
a very slight thickness would suffice. The youth of either sex
might by this means sleep, as well as study, under inspection,
and alone – a circumstance of no mean importance in many
a parent's eye.

In the Royal Military School at Paris, the bed-chambers (if
my brother's memory does not deceive him) form two ranges on
the two sides of a long room; the inhabitants being separated
from one another by *partitions*, but exposed alike to the view of
a master at his walks, by a kind of a *grated window* in each door.
This plan of construction struck him, he tells me, a good deal,
as he walked over that establishment (about a dozen years ago,
was it not?) with you; and possibly in that walk the foundation
was laid for his Inspection-House. If he there borrowed his idea,
I hope he has not repaid it without interest. You will confess
some difference, in point of facility, betwixt a state of incessant
walking and a state of rest; and in point of completeness
of inspection, between visiting two or three hundred persons
one after another, and seeing them at once.

In stating what this principle *will* do in promoting the
progress of instruction in every line, a word or two will
be thought sufficient to state what it will *not* do. It *does* give
every degree of efficacy which can be given to the influence of
punishment and *restraint*. But it does nothing towards correct-
ing the oppressive influence of punishment and restraint,

by the enlivening and invigorating influence of *reward*. That noblest and brightest engine of discipline can by no other means be put to constant use in schools, than by the practice which at Westminster, you know, goes by the name of *challenging* – an institution which, paying merit in its fittest and most inexhaustible coin, and even uniting in one impulse the opposite powers of reward and punishment, holds out dishonour for every attention a boy omits, and honour for every exertion he can bestow.

With regard to the extending the range of inspection over every moment of a boy's time, the sentiments of mankind might not be altogether so unanimous. The notion, indeed, of most parents is, I believe, that children cannot be too much under the master's eye; and if man were a consistent animal, none who entertain that notion but should be fonder of the principle the farther they saw it pursued. But as consistency is of all human qualities the most rare, it need not at all surprise us, if, of those who in the present state of things are most anxious on the head of the master's omnipresence, many were to fly back and change their note, when they saw that point screwed up at once to a pitch of perfection so much beyond whatever they could have been accustomed to conceive.

Some there are, at any rate, who, before they came into so novel a scheme, would have many scruples to get over. Doubts would be started – Whether it would be advisable to apply such constant and unremitting pressure to the tender mind, and to give such herculean and ineludible strength to the gripe of power? – whether persons, of the cast of character and extent of ideas that may be expected to be found in the common run of schoolmasters, are likely to be fit receptacles for an authority so much exceeding anything that has been hitherto signified by *despotic?* – whether the *in*-attention of the master may not be as necessary to the *present* comfort of his *pupil*, in some respects, as the attention of the one may be to the *future* welfare of the other, in other respects? – whether the irretrievable check given to the free development of the intellectual part of his frame by this unintermitted pressure, may not be productive of an imbecility similar to that which would be produced by constant and long-continued *bandages* on the corporeal part? – whether what is thus acquired in *regularity* may not be lost in *energy?* – whether that not less instructive, though less heeded, course of discipline, which in the struggles of passion against passion, and of reason against reason, is administered by the children to one another and to themselves, and in which the conflicts and competitions that are to form the business of maturity are rehearsed in miniature; whether I say, this moral and most important branch of instruction would not by these means be sacrificed to the rudiments, and those seldom the most useful, of the intellectual? – whether the defects, with which *private* education has been charged in its comparison with public, would not here be carried to the extreme? – and whether, in being made a little better acquainted with the world of abstraction than they might have been otherwise, the youth thus pent up may not have been kept more than proportionably ignorant of the world of realities into which they are about to launch? – whether the liberal spirit and energy of a free citizen would not be exchanged for the mechanical discipline of a soldier, or the austerity of a monk? – and whether the result of this high-wrought contrivance might not be constructing a set of *machines* under the similitude of *men?*

To give a satisfactory answer to all these queries, which are mighty fine, but do not any of them come home to the point, it would be necessary to recur at once to the end of education. Would *happiness* be most likely to be increased or diminished by this discipline? – Call them soldiers, call them monks, call them machines: so they were but happy ones, I should not care. Wars and storms are best to read of, but peace and calms are better to enjoy. Don't be frightened now, my dear *****, and think that I am going to entertain you with a course of moral philosophy, or even with a system of education. Happiness is a very pretty thing to feel, but very dry to talk about; so you may unknit your brow, for I shall say no more about the matter. One thing only I will add, which is, that whoever sets up an inspection-school upon the tiptop of the principle, had need to be very sure of the master; for the boy's body is not more the child of his father's, than his mind will be of the master's mind; with no other difference than what there is between *command* on one side and *subjection* on the other.

Some of these fine queries which I have been treating you

with, and finer still, Rousseau would have entertained us with; nor do I imagine he would have put his *Emilius* into an inspection-house; but I think he would have been glad of such a school for his Sophia.

Addison, the grave and moral Addison, in his *Spectator* or his *Tatler*, I forget which, suggests a contrivance for trying *virginity* by means of *lions*. You may there find many curious disquisitions concerning the measures and degrees of that species of purity; all which you will be better pleased to have from that grave author than from me. But, without plunging into any such discussions, the highest degree possible, whatsoever that may be, is no more than anybody might make sure of, only by transferring damsels at as early an age as may be thought sufficient, into a strict inspection-school. Addison's scheme was not only a penal but a bloody one: and what havoc it might have made in the population of the country, I tremble but to think of. Give thanks, then, to *Diana* and the *eleven thousand virgins*, and to whatever powers preside over virginity in either *calendar*, for so happy a discovery as this of your friend's. There you saw blood and uncertainty: here you see certainty without blood. What advantage might be made by setting up a boarding-school for young ladies upon this plan, and with what eagerness gentlemen who are curious in such matters would crowd to such a school to choose themselves wives, is too obvious to insist on. The only inconvenience I can think of is, that if the institution were to become general, Mrs. Ch. H. and other gentlewomen of her calling, would be obliged either to give up house-keeping, or take up with low wenches or married ladies.

Dr. Brown the estimator would have been stark mad for an inspection-school upon the very extremity of the principle, provided always he were to have been head-master, and then he would have had no other schools but those. His antagonist, Dr. Priestly, would, I imagine, be altogether as averse to it, unless, perhaps, for experiment's sake, upon a small scale, just enough to furnish an appendix to *Hartley upon Man*.

You have a controversy, I find, in England, about *Sunday-schools*. Schools upon the extremity of the inspection-principle would, I am apt to think, find more advocates among the patrons than among the oppugners of that measure.

We are told, somewhere or other, of a King of Egypt (*Psammitichus*, I think, is his name) who thinking to re-discover the lost original of language, contrived to breed up two children in a sequestered spot, secluded, from the hour of birth, from all converse with the rest of humankind. No great matters were, I believe, collected from this experiment. An inspection-house, to which a set of children had been consigned from their birth, might afford experiments enough that would be rather more interesting. What say you to a *foundling-hospital* upon this principle? Would ****'s *manes* give you leave to let your present school and build another upon this ground? If I do not misrecollect, your brethren in that trust have gone so far as to make a point, where it can be effected, of taking the children out of the hands of their parents as much as possible, and even, if possible, altogether. If you have gone thus far, you have passed the Rubicon; you may even clap them up in an inspection-house, and they you make of them what you please. You need never grudge the parents *a peep behind the curtain* in the master's lodge. There, as often as they had a mind, they might see their children thriving and learning, if that would satisfy them, without interrupting business or counteracting discipline. Improving upon Psam-mitichus's experiment, you might keep up a sixteen or eighteen years separation between the male and female part of your young subjects; and at the end of that period see what the language of love would be, when *Father Francis's Ganders* were turned into *Father Francis's Geese*.

I know who would have been delighted to set up an inspection-school, if it were only for the experiment's sake, and that is Helvetius: at least, if he had been steady to his principles, which he was said to be: for by that contrivance, and by that alone, he might have been enabled to give an experimental proof of the truth of his position (supposing it to be true) that anybody may be taught anything, one person as well as another. It would have been his fault, if what he requires as a condition, viz. that the subjects of the experiment be placed in circumstances exactly similar, were not fulfilled.

A rare field of discovery in *metaphysics:* a science which, now for the first time, may be put to the test of experiment, like any other. Books, conversation, sensible objects, everything, might

be *given*. The genealogy of each observable idea might be traced
through all its degrees with the utmost nicety: the parent stocks
being all known and numbered. Party men, controversialists
of every description, and all other such epicures, whose mouth
waters at the mammon of power, might here give themselves
a rich treat, adapted to their several tastes, unembittered
by contradiction. Two and two might here be less than four, or
the moon might be made of green cheese; if any pious founder,
who were rich enough, chose to have her of that material.
Surrounded by a circle of pupils, obsequious beyond anything
as yet known under the name of obsequiousness, their happiness
might in such a mansion be complete, if any moderate number
of adherents could content them; which unhappily is not
the case. At the end of some twenty or five-and-twenty years,
introduce the scholars of the different schools to one another
(observing first to tie their hands behind them) and you will see
good sport; though perhaps you may think there is enough
of that kind of sport already. But if you throw out this hint to
anybody, you will take care, as far as sects and religions are
concerned, not to mention names; for of these, how few are
there but would be ready to pull us to pieces, if they saw their
rivals set down upon the same line, as candidates for the same
advantage? And this is what we should get by our impartiality.
– You may, however, venture to hint, that the money which
is now laid out for propagating controversy, by founding
sermons and lectures, might be laid out with greater certainty
of advantage in the founding *controversial inspection-schools*.
The preachers must be sad bunglers, indeed, if they had not
there as many adherents as auditors; which is not always
the case in the world at large. As to flagellation, and other such
ceremonies, which more through custom than necessity
are used by way of punishment in schools, but which under
some institutions form the *routine* of life, I need not take up
your time in showing how much the punctuality of those trans-
actions might, in the latter case, be improved by the inspection
principle. These monastic accomplishments have not been in
fashion in our country for some ages: – therefore it would be lost
labour to recommend the principle in that view. Neither are
they a whit more so where I write; so that I should get as little
thanks for my pains, were I to make such a proposal here.

On the contrary, we are dissolving monasteries as you would lumps of sugar. A lump, for instance, we got the other day at Kieff, enough to feed a brace of regiments, besides pickings for other people. But if in my return to England, or at any other time, I should happen to go by the monastery of *La Trappe*, or any other where they are in earnest about such business, it would be cruelty to deny them the assistance it might be made to receive from the inspection principle. *Flinching* would then be as impracticable in a monastery, as *cribbing* in a school. Old scores might thus be rubbed out with as much regularity as could be desired; nor would the pride of *Toboso* have been so long a-disenchanting, could her *Knight* have put his coward *Squire* into an inspection-house.

Neither do I mean to give any instructions to the *Turks* for applying the inspection principle to their *seraglios*: no, not though I were to go through Constantinople again twenty times, notwithstanding the great saving it would make in the article of *eunuchs*, of whom one trusty one in the inspection-lodge would be as good as half a hundred. The price of that kind of cattle could not fail of falling at least ten per cent., and the insurance upon marital honour at least as much, upon the bare hint given of such an establishment in any of the Constantinople papers. But the mobbing I got at *Shoomlo*, only for taking a peep at the town from a thing they call a *minaret* (like our monument) in pursuance of invitation, has cancelled any claims they might have had upon me for the dinner they gave me at the *divan*, had it been better than it was.

If the idea of some of these applications should have brought a smile upon your countenance, it won't hurt you, my dear ****; nor should it hurt the principle. Your candour will prevent you from condemning a great and new invented instrument of government, because some of the purposes to which it is possible to apply it may appear useless, or trifling, or mischievous, or ridiculous. Its great excellence consists in the great strength it is capable of giving to *any* institution it may be thought proper to apply it to. If any perverse applications should ever be made of it, they will lie in this case as in others, at the doors of those who make them. Knives, however sharp, are very useful things, and, for most purposes, the sharper the more useful. I have no fear, therefore, of your wishing to forbid the use of them, because they have been sometimes employed by school-boys *to raise the devil* with, or by assassins to cut throats with.

I hope no critic of more learning than candour will do an inspection-house so much injustice as to compare it to *Dionysius' ear*. The object of that contrivance was, to know what prisoners said without their suspecting any such thing. The object of the inspection principle is directly the reverse: it is to make them not only *suspect,* but be *assured,* that whatever they do is known, even though that should not be the case. Detection is the object of the first: *prevention,* that of the latter. In the former case the ruling person is a spy; in the latter he is a monitor. The object of the first was to pry into the secret recesses of the heart; the latter, confining its attention to *overt acts,* leaves thoughts and fancies to their proper *ordinary,* the court *above.*

When I consider the extensive variety of purposes to which this principle may be applied, and the certain efficacy which, as far as I can trust my own conceptions, it promises to them all, my wonder is, not only that this plan should never have hitherto been put in practice, but how any other should ever have been thought of.

In so many edifices, as, from the time of the conquest to the present, have been built for the express purpose of safe custody, does it sound natural that, instead of placing the prisoners under the inspection of their keepers, the one class should have been lodged at one end, perhaps, of a vast building, and the other at another end? – as if the object of the establishment were, that those who wished to escape might carry on their schemes in concert, and at leisure. I should suppose the inspection principle must long ago have occurred to the ingenious, and been rejected by the judicious, could I, after all my efforts, conceive a reason for the rejection. The circular form, notwithstanding its taking demonstrably less materials than any other, may, for aught I know, on its first construction, be more expensive than one of equal dimensions in any of the ordinary forms. But this objection, which has no other source than the loose and random surmise of one who has had no experience in building, can never have held good in comparison with all the other prisons that we have, if in truth it holds good in comparison with any. Witness the massy piles of Newgate, of which the enormous, and upon the common plans by no means unnecessary expense, has been laid out in the purchase of a degree of security, not equal to that which the circular form would have given to the slightest building that could be made to hold together. In short, as often as I indulge myself in the liberty of fancying that my own notions on this head may prove conformable to other people's, I think of the old story of *Columbus* and his *egg*.

I have now set this *egg* of ours on its end: – whether it will stand fast, and bear the shocks of discussion, remains to be decided by experience. I think you will not find it stale; but its freshness is a circumstance, that may not give it an equal relish to every palate.

What would you say, if by the gradual adoption and diversified application of this single principle, you should see a new scene of things spread itself over the face of civilized society? – morals reformed, health preserved, industry invigorated, instruction diffused, public burthens lightened, economy seated as it were upon a rock, the gordian knot of the poor-laws not cut but untied – all by a simple idea in architecture?*

I am, &c.

---

* This plan happened not to come in time for the particular purpose it was designed for.

POSTSCRIPT, PART I.

CONTAINING

FURTHER PARTICULARS AND ALTERATIONS
RELATIVE TO THE PLAN OF CONSTRUCTION
ORIGINALLY PROPOSED;

PRINCIPALLY ADAPTED TO THE PURPOSE OF A

PANOPTICON PENITENTIARY-HOUSE.*

SECTION VII.
CHAPEL.
*Chapel Introduced.***

THE necessity of a chapel to a penitentiary-house, is a point
rather to be assumed than argued. Under an established
church of any persuasion, a system of penitence without the
means of regular devotion, would be a downright solecism. If
religious instruction and exercise be not necessary to the
worst, and generally the most ignorant of sinners, to whom
else can they be other than superfluous?

This instruction, where then shall they be placed to receive
it? Nowhere better than where they are. There they are in
a state of continued safe custody; and there they are without
any additional expense. It remains only to place the chaplain;
and where the chaplain is, there is the chapel. A speaker

---

* Originally printed in 1791.

** The chapel, not being a characteristic part of the design, will be sufficiently
understood from the draught, without any particular explanation. For the
whole detail of this part, I am indebted to my professional adviser, Mr. Revely,
of Great Titchfield Street, Marybone, whose beautiful and correct drawings of
views in the Levant have been so much admired by the dilettanti in Grecian
and Egyptian antiquities.

cannot be distinctly heard more than a very few feet behind the spot he speaks from.* The congregation being placed in a circle, the situation, therefore, of the chaplain should be, not in the centre of that circle, but as near as may be to that part which is behind him, and, consequently, at the greatest distance from that part of it to which he turns his face.

But between the centre of the inspection-tower all round, and the intermediate well, there must be, at any rate, whatever use it may be put to, a very considerable space. What, then, shall be done with it? It cannot be employed as a warehouse consistently with the sanctity of its destination; nor even independently of that consideration, since, if thus filled up, it would intercept both sight and voice. Even if divine service were out of the question, it is only towards the centre that this part could be employed for stowage, without obstructing inspection as much as in the other case it would devotion; nor can it, even in that part, be so employed, without narrowing in proportion the inspector's range, and protruding his walk to a longer and longer circuit. What, then, shall we do with this vacuity? Fill it with company, if company can be induced to come. Why not, as well as to the Asylum, the Magdalen, and the Lock Hospital, in London? The scene would be more picturesque; the occasion not less interesting and affecting. The prospect of contributions that might be collected here as there, will bind the manager to the observance of every rule that can contribute to keep the establishment in a state of exemplary neatness and cleanliness, while the profit of them will pay him for the expense and trouble. Building, furniture, apparel, persons, every thing, must be kept as nice as a Dutch house. The smallest degree of ill scent would be fatal to this part of his enterprise. To give it success, prejudices indeed would be to be surmounted; but by experience – continued and uninterrupted experience – even prejudice may be overcome.

The affluence of visitors, while it secured cleanliness, and its concomitants healthiness and good order, would keep up a system of gratuitous inspection, capable of itself of awing the keeper into good conduct, even if he were not paid for it: and

---

* I found this by experiments made on purpose in churches. See also Saunders on Theatres.

the opposite impulses of hope and fear would thus contribute to ensure perfection to the management, and keep the conduct of the manager wound up to the highest pitch of duty. Add to this the benefit of the example, and of the comments that would be made on it by learned and religious lips: these seeds of virtue, instead of being buried in obscurity, as in other improved prisons, would thus be disseminated far and wide.

Whatever profit, if any, the contractor could make out of this part of the plan, why grudge it him? why to his establishment, more than to any of those just mentioned? Not a penny of it but would be a bounty upon good management, and a security against abuse.

If the furniture and decoration of the chapel would require some expense, though very little decoration would be requisite, a saving, on the other hand, results from the degree of openness which such a destination suggested and rendered necessary. On the original plan, the whole circuit of the central part, then appropriated solely to inspection, was to have been filled with glass: on the present plan, which lays this part open in different places, to the amount of at least half its height, that expensive material is proportionately saved.

On the present plan, it will be observed, that three stories of cells only, viz. the second, third, and fifth from the top, enjoy an uninterrupted view of the minister.* That the inhabitants of the other stories of cells may have participation of the same benefit, it will be necessary they should be introduced, for the occasion, into or in front of such of the cells as are in a situation to enjoy it. This might be effected, and that with the greatest ease, were the whole establishment to receive even a *double complement.*

The two parties, composed of the fixed inhabitants of each cell on the one hand, and the strangers imported from a distant cell on the other, might be stationed either in one continued row in the front of the cell-galleries, or the one party in that line, and the other immediately within the cell-grating. In neither case need the law of seclusion be suffered to be infringed by

---

* In some impressions of the draught, the minister's station, and, consequently, the views and want of views that result from it, are not represented: but they will readily be conceived.

converse: both parties are alike awed to silence by an invisible eye – invisible not only to the prisoners in front, but to the company behind: not only the person of each inspector, but his very station, being perfectly concealed from every station in the chapel.*

---

* All this may be very well, said an intelligent friend, in the way of *example:* – but how stands it upon the footing of *reformation?* Might it not have ultimately a corruptive effect upon the persons thus exhibited, – shaming them, indeed, and distressing them at first, but by degrees hardening them, and at length rendering them insensible? Would it not, in short, to this purpose, be a sort of perpetual pillory?

To this I answer –

1. That, of the two, example and reformation, example is the greatest object; and that in the proportion of the number of the yet innocent to that of the convicted guilty.

2. That the offences for which persons are subjected to this punishment are deemed of a deeper dye, and as such to require a punishment more severe than that even of those who are consigned to the pillory.

3. That at their trials there is not one of them but must have been exhibited in a manner equally public, and in circumstances reflecting a much greater measure of humiliation and shame: with this difference too, that on that occasion each person is exhibited singly, and the eyes of the whole audience are fixed upon him alone: that he is to speak as well as to hear, and stands forth in effect the sole hero of the melancholy drama: whereas, on an exhibition like that here proposed, the attention of the spectators, being divided among so many, scarcely attaches individually upon any one. Besides that upon his trial a man is held forth to view with the marks of guilt fresh upon his head: whereas at the remote period in question he does not appear till a progress more or less considerable may be presumed to have been made in the career of penitence, and the idea of guilt has been covered by expiation.

Should these answers be thought not to have disproved the mischief, nothing can be simpler than the remedy. A mask affords it at once. Guilt will thus be pilloried in the abstract, without the exposure of the guilty. With regard to the sufferer, the sting of shame will be sheathed, and with regard to the spectators, the salutary impression, instead of being weakened, will be heightened, by this imagery. The scene of devotion will be decorated by – why mince the word? – by a masquerade: a masquerade, indeed, but of what kind? not a gay and dangerous, but a serious, affecting, and instructive one. A Spanish *auto-da-fe* has still more in it of the theatre: – and what is the objection there? That the spectacle is light or ludicrous? No: but rather that it is too serious and too horrible.

This, it is to be noted, is the only occasion on which their eyes will have to encounter the public eye. At all other times, be their visitors ever so numerous, there will be no consciousness of being seen, consequently no ground for the insensibility which might be apprehended from the habit of such consciousness.

Where there is patience to discriminate, the worst institutions may afford a hint that may be of use. I would not turn my back upon reason and utility, though I found them in the Starchamber or the Inquisition. The authors of the latter institution, in particular, whatever enormities and absurdities may

SECTION VIII.
INSPECTION-GALLERIES AND LODGE.

IN the three stories of the inspection-tower, annular inspection-galleries, low and narrow, surrounding in the lowermost story a circular inspection-lodge; instead of three stories of inspection-lodge, all circular, and in height filling up the whole space all the way up.*

Two desiderata had been aimed at in the contrivance of the inspector's stations: 1. The unbounded faculty of seeing without being seen, and that as well while moving to and fro, as while sitting or standing still: 2. The capacity of receiving in the same place visitors who should be in the same predicament.

The second of these objects is not to be dispensed with. If the governor or sub-governor cannot, for the purposes of his business, receive company while he remains in this station, he must, as often as he receives them, quit not only the central part, but the whole circle altogether, leaving his place in the inspection part to be supplied by somebody on purpose. Hence, on the one hand, a relaxation of the inspective force: on the other, an increase in the expense of management.

---

be laid to their charge, must at least be allowed to have had some knowledge of *stage effect*. Unjust as was their penal system in its application, and barbarous in its degree, the skill they displayed in making the most of it in point of impression, their solemn processions, their emblematic dresses, their terrific scenery, deserve rather to be admired and imitated than condemned.

Nihil ex scenâ, says Lord Bacon, speaking of procedure in the civil branch of the law: *Multum ex scenâ*, I will venture to say, speaking of the penal. The disagreement is but verbal: *Scena*, in the language of the noble philosopher, means *lying:* in mine, *scena* is but *scenery*. To say, *Multum ex scenâ*, is to say, lose no occasion of speaking to the eye. In a well-composed committee of penal law, I know not a more essential personage than the manager of a theatre.

*It is to the ingenuity of Mr. Revely that I am indebted for this very capital improvement, which I did not submit to without reluctance. It occurred to him in contriving the construction of the chapel, in the room of some crude ideas of my own, a detailed description of which would take up more room than it would be worth. The floors of the present inspector's galleries were to have been continued inwards as far as what constitutes now the area of the chapel. The governor and his subordinates were to have lived in them on week days, and on Sundays these floors were to have answered the purpose of galleries to the chapel. All the way up from floor to floor there were to have been windows, which were to have been got rid of somehow or other during the time of divine service.

Suppose it possible, as I conceive it will be found, for the inspector's invisibility to be preserved, upon condition of giving up that of the visitors, would the former advantage be sufficient without the latter? Not absolutely: for confederates, as the discrimination could not well be made, might gain entrance in numbers at a time, and while one was occupying the attention of the inspector, others might by signs concert enterprises of mischief or escape with the prisoners in their cells. Such, at least, might be the apprehension entertained by some people – at least upon the face of this single supposition; though to one whose conception should have embraced the whole system of safeguard and defence, the danger would, I think, hardly appear formidable enough to warrant the incurring any expense, or sacrificing any advantage.

Upon the first crude conception, as stated in the Letters, my hope had been, that by the help of blinds and screens, the faculty of invisible inspection might have been enjoyed in perfection by the whole number of persons occupying the central part, wherever they were placed in it, and whether in motion or at rest. I am now assured, and I fear with truth, that these expectations were in some respects too sanguine. I mean, as to what concerns ideal and absolute perfection: at the same time that for real service, their completion, I trust, will not be found to have sustained any material abatement.

Were I to persist in endeavouring to give this property of invisibility with regard to the cells, as well to the person of the inspector as to every part of the large circle in which I place him, and to every object in it, his situation would stand exposed, I am assured, to this dilemma if he has light enough to do any business, he will be seen, whatever I can do, from the cells: if there is not light enough there for him to be seen from the cells, there will not be light enough to enable him to do his business.

The difficulty would not be removed, even though the chapel part in the centre were thrown out, and the inspector's apartment extended so as to swallow up that central part, and occupy the whole circle. My expedient of diametrical screens, or partitions crossing each other at right angles, would not answer the purpose:* if they extended all the way from the

---

* See Letter II.

circumference to the centre, leaving no vacuity at that part, they would divide the whole circle into separate quadrants: a man could be in but one of these quadrants at a time, and while he was in that one he could see nothing of the cells corresponding to the others. Stationed exactly in the centre, he would see indeed, but he could at the same time be seen from, all the cells at once. No space can ever be so exactly closed as to exclude the light, by any living figure.

Supposing the apertures I had contrived in the screens instead of doors capable of answering the purpose, they would leave to the lodge so provided but little if any advantage over an annular gallery at the extremity of the circle, as contrived by Mr. Revely. The circuit might be performed nearer the centre; but still, to carry on the process of inspection, a circuit must be performed. Nor could it be performed in an exact circle: the smaller circle thus meant to be performed would be broken in upon and lengthened in four places by zigzags, which would retard a man's progress more than an equal length of circle, and might, upon the whole, consume a portion of time little less than what would be requisite for performing the perambulation in Mr. Revely's inspection-galleries.*

Add to this, that the darkness thus spread over the station

---

* The truth is, what one would hardly have supposed, that for performing this perambulation, a walk of about 46 feet and back again in a straight line, is pretty well sufficient. Station the inspector anywhere with his eye contiguous to the outer circumference of his ring, he can, without quitting the spot he stands or sits on, command a view of seven cells on each side. In the same ring, 46 feet may be described in walking without deviating from the right line: and 46 feet is the length of the chord subtending the space occupied in the circumference by 5 cells. A walk, then, in a line equal and opposite to the chord subtending the part of the gallery that corresponds to the dead-part, will give an inspector in his gallery a view of the whole circuit. If, as in case of the admission of female prisoners, the circuit be divided in any story between a male and female inspector, the part allotted to each may, it is evident, be commanded without any change of place. The views thus obtained are not, it must be confessed, complete ones: more or less of every cell but two being all along intercepted by the partition-walls. But it is chance only, and not design, that can withdraw a prisoner in any part of the circuit out of the inspector's view: never knowing in what part of the gallery the inspector is at the time, no one part of any cell can promise him any better chance of concealment than another.

The calculation, it is to be observed, is taken from the real design: were the measurement to be performed upon the engraving, the result, owing to the error already mentioned, would be still more favourable.

of the inspector would not admit of any cure. A candle could not be made to illuminate any object he had occasion to see, without throwing out rays that would render him more or less visible, and his situation and occupation more or less apparent, from the cells. If a screen, concentric to the circumference of the room, were anywhere interposed, and light admitted within side of it by a sky-light or void space over the centre of the building, that would increase the length of the zigzag circuit to be performed through the diametrical screens still more: if there were no such concentric screens, the thorough light would be completely let in, rendering the inspector and every other object in the room completely visible from all the cells.

Happily, this union of incompatible conditions, however requisite to fill up the measure of ideal perfection, is far from being so with regard to practical use. In the narrow annular gallery, as contrived by Mr. Revely, the condition of invisibility may be preserved, I am assured, in full perfection. By being painted black in the inside, that station may be rendered, by the help of blinds, as I had proposed, completely dark, its narrowness rendering it impermeable to the thorough light.

To change his prospect, the inspector must, it is true, be obliged to shift his station. He must therefore from time to time patrol and go his round in the manner of a centinel or a watchman: and this must form a considerable part of his employment. It need not, however, occupy any thing near the whole.* Stationed at no more than 28 or 29 feet from the exterior windows, and close to the space illuminated by the ample skylight over the annular well, he would have light enough to read or write by: and these employments, by the help of a portable stool and desk, he might carry on at times, at any part of the circle. Books may be kept, entries made, as well in a room of an annular figure, as in a round or square one.

Nor will the time employed in perambulation be thrown away, or expended upon the single purpose of keeping order among the prisoners. Had he, instead of this ring, had the whole circle to range in, he would have had frequent occasion thus to travel in the circumference, were it only to give occasional

---

* The greatest distance from one part of his range to the other would be 93 feet, being half the length of the circumference of the circle at that part.

orders and instructions to the prisoners as they sit at work in their cells, as well as to let them in and out, in manner already mentioned.*

One expedient there remains, by which, if it be worth while, the invisibility of the inspector may be preserved to him, without the obligation of ever stirring from his seat. This, however, is subject to two restrictions: one is, that whenever he quits a particular spot in the room, to pass to any other part of the same room, he must become visible; the other is, that his invisibility is not shared by any other person in the room. The expedient is to place the inspector in a kind of lantern, shaped somewhat like two short-necked funnels joined together at their necks.

Placed as before on a floor situated midway between the floor and the ceiling of the lowermost of the two stories he commands, his light comes to him from a spot elevated above the eye of a person standing in the uppermost of those stories; consequently, in all cases above the eye of any person dwelling in that upper story. Level with his eye, whether sitting or standing, the lantern narrows to such a degree as to enable him to carry his eye close to the circumference all round, without changing the spot he sits or stands on.

To give him his view, the lantern is pierced at both elevations with small holes, corresponding, as upon trial shall be found most convenient, each of them to one or two or some greater number of the cells. These holes are no larger than the

---

* See Sect. 3, *Annular Well*, and Part II. Sect. *Airing*.

Your occasional vigilance will not do, says an objector: *Your prisoner will make experiments upon it, discover when Argus nods, and make his advantage of the discovery. He will hazard a venial transgression at a venture: that un-noticed, he will go on to more material ones.* Will he? I will soon put an end to his experiments: or rather, to be beforehand with him, I will take care he shall not think of making any. I will single out one of the most untoward of the prisoners. I will keep an unintermitted watch upon him. I will watch until I observe a transgression. I will minute it down. I will wait for another: I will note that down too. I will lie by for a whole day: he shall do as he pleases that day, so long as he does not venture at something too serious to be endured. The next day I produce the list to him. – *You thought yourself undiscovered: you abused my indulgence: see how you were mistaken. Another time, you may have rope for two days, ten days: the longer it is, the heavier it will fall upon you. Learn from this, all of you, that in this house transgression never can be safe.* Will the policy be cruel? – No; it will be kind: it will prevent transgressing; it will save punishing.

aperture of a common spying-glass, and, like that, closed by a piece of glass, which if necessary might be coloured, or smoked, or darkened by a blind. Grant that after all they will not perfectly exclude the thorough light, nor prevent his figure from being to a certain degree visible from the cells: still, however, the part of his figure thus betrayed will be so small, that to the purpose of discovering to a prisoner in his cell whether the eye of the inspector is at that moment directed towards him or not, it will be the same thing as if he were invisible. That by diminishing the apertures to a certain degree, the effect might be compassed, is indubitable; for the lantern might be of the thinness of paper: in short, it might in that part be of paper, and then a pin-hole would be sufficient to give him a view. Any opaque object, to let down by a line and pulley on his going out, would prevent his absence from being discernible. The difference between a body of that magnitude constantly at rest, and one occasionally in motion, would be masked by the smallness of the apertures.

At the altitude reaching between the height of his eye when sitting, and the height of his eye when standing, the lantern could not be too narrow: it should be only just wide enough to admit his head and shoulders with ease. Above and below that height, the wider the better, for the sake of air and room, so as it did not swell out in such manner as to intercept his view.

The next question is, how to prevent the prisoners from seeing when it is he quits his station? His exit and return, if performed by a door in the side, would be visible from all, or almost all the cells – his lantern not serving him in the capacity of a screen on such occasions, to any degree worth mentioning. To prevent such discovery, his entrance must be, not at an ordinary door on the side, but at a trap-door, by a ladder from below. The lantern might, however, besides that, be furnished with a door at the side, to give him passage at times, when the concealment of his situation was no longer material, and when he saw occasion to show himself for any purpose to the inhabitants of any particular cell: for instance, to give a prisoner passage to or from his cell, for the purpose and in the manner already mentioned.

The central aperture, large as it is, would be no bar to the employing of this contrivance. The lantern, it is true, could not occupy this central part: it must be placed somewhere on one side of it, in some part of some surrounding ring. The inspector, therefore, while stationed in this lantern, would not have a view equally near of all his cells; but of all he would have some view, and that, one may venture to say, a sufficient one: the difference would only be the distance from the centre of the lantern to the centre of the building; say from ten to a dozen feet. The part, too, from which he was in this manner farthest removed, might be the dead-part, where there are no cells – a division which, upon the present plan, occupies five parts in twenty-four of the whole circuit.

Still, however, an apartment thus circumstanced would not serve perfectly well for visitors; for they, at any rate, would be visible to the prisoners: which, for the reasons already mentioned, it were better they should not be. Here, then, comes in one use of the inspector's lodge, a room situated within the inspection-gallery, and encircled by it all round. Many other uses, and those very material, will be observed in it, when the construction has been described; uses, to which, it will be equally manifest that a transparent room, fitted up with an inspection-lantern, would not be applicable with advantage.

The inspector's lodge is a circular, or rather annular apartment, immediately underneath the chapel. The diameter I propose now to give it is 54 feet, including the aperture in the centre.*

The central aperture in this story is of the same diameter, as in the area of the chapel and the dome that crowns it, viz. 12 feet: it serves here to light the centre of the *diametrical passage,* of which, under the head of *communications.* This aperture is likewise of farther use in the way of safeguard; for which also see the head of *communications.*

---

* In some of the impressions of the draught it appears but 42 feet: difference 12 feet. But of this, six feet is taken away from this part by an error in the draught, as already mentioned: the other six feet, by the three feet added to the depth of the inspection-gallery in this story – an addition which I have determined to take away: it has no specific use; and it would throw the lodge so far back as to be precluded by the bottom of the middlemost inspection-gallery from the possibility of having any view at all of the uppermost story of cells.

As the central aperture in the floor of the lodge gives light to the passage in the story underneath, so does the correspondent aperture in the area of the chapel give light to the lodge.

Of these central apertures, that which is in the floor of the chapel takes nothing of the room from visitors. During chapel times it is closed: the state of darkness to which it thereby reduces the lodge is then of no consequence, since at those times nobody is there. So likewise, in a cold winter's evening, when day-light gives place to candle-light, the faculty of closing this aperture will probably be found to have its convenience. Its height, at the circumference, is that of the inspection-gallery, about 7 feet; at the central aperture about 13½ feet;* within that aperture, about 61 feet, that being the depth below the sky-light by which the central apertures are crowned. The ceiling is consequently a sloping one; dropping, in the course of 18 feet, about 6½ feet, viz. from 13½ to 7.

All round the circuit, the dead-part excepted, runs a narrow zone of window, to open to the lodge an occasional view of the cells. Of these, the two lower stories may be seen through the lowermost inspection-gallery; the others without any intermedium.

The ways in which this view might be opened are more than one: the simplest is to put two rows of panes; one for giving a view of the two lowermost stories of cells, a little below the highest part of the upright partition: the other for the four remaining stories, in the chord subtending the angle made by the junction of that partition with the ceiling. To these may be adapted blinds of coarse white muslin or linen, pierced every inch or two with eyelet holes about the size of an ordinary silver spangle. By this means, matters may unquestionably be ordered in some way or other, so that no view at all shall be obtainable in the cells of any thing that passes in the lodge; at the same time that a person in the lodge may, by applying his eye close to any of the holes, obtain a perfectly distinct view of the corresponding cells.

By the central aperture, were that all, a moderately good

---

* The draught does not give quite so much. The higher the better, so long as it does not raise the floor of the chapel so much as that the heads of the chapel visitors, when standing, shall conceal the minister from the prisoners when kneeling in the second story of cells.

light, it is supposed, would be afforded to the lodge: and this light cannot but receive some addition from the luminous zone thus given to the circumference.*

To gain the height at which the business of inspection can in this manner be occasionally performed from the lodge, an ascent of about 1½ or 2 feet must be made: this may be done by a circular bench of about 2 feet wide, attached all round to the partition-wall. It may be distinguished by the name of the *inspection-platform* or *inspection-bench*.

By means of the lower part of this zone, the inspector of the gallery attached may himself be inspected by his superiors from the lodge: reciprocity will be prevented by the advantage in height given to the commanding station. He may also be relieved at any time; and whenever the windows of the gallery are thrown open for air, the lodge succeeds, in a manner of course, to its inspection-powers; the view brightening of itself at the time when a view particularly clear is more particularly wanted. So, likewise, when the inspector in the gallery is obliged to show himself at any particular spot; for instance, by opening the door of one of the cells, losing thereby his omnipresence for the time.**

The lodge is the heart, which gives life and motion to this artificial body: hence issue all *orders*: here centre all *reports*.

The conversation-tubes, spoken of in the Letters, will on this occasion be recollected: here they will find employment in more shapes than one.

One set is for holding converse with the subordinate

---

* The Pantheon at Rome, which is more than twice the height of the space between the floor of the lodge and the opening sky-light over the aperture, is lighted, and, according to Mr. Revely's observation, very well lighted, by an aperture of about twice the diameter of the one here proposed.

** In a panopticon which had eight stories of cells, it might perhaps be not amiss to make the experiment of the lantern. It might be performed on a floor between the lodge and the chapel; the ladder or small staircase to it, like that of a pulpit, ascending through the ceiling of the lodge. It might be tried at a small expense: and in case of its not answering, it would be easy to give to this story the form of the other. Possibly, in different ways, both arrangements might have their use.

But the sorts of panopticons to which the contrivance of the lantern is more particularly adapted, are those in which seclusion from society would be out of the question; such as houses of industry, free manufactories, or schools.

inspectors in the two superior galleries. A small tube of tin or copper* passes from the lodge, in a horizontal direction, to one of the supports of the lowermost inspection-gallery, running immediately underneath the roof, to which it is attached by rings. Here, bending to a right angle, it runs up along the support till it reaches that one of the two superior galleries for which it is designed: it there terminates in a mouth-piece level with the ear or mouth of a person sitting there. A similar mouth-piece is fitted to it at its commencement in the lodge.

A tube of this sort for each gallery may be attached to every one, or every other one, of the 19 gallery-supports, corresponding to the number of the cells.

The tubes belonging to the different stories should be attached together in pairs, with their respective mouth-pieces in the lodge contiguous, that a superior in that apartment may have it in his power to hold converse with the subordinates of the two different galleries at the same time, without being under the necessity of vibrating all the while from place to place.

Whether the voice alone will be sufficient, or whether a bell will be necessary, to summon a subordinate inspector from the most distant part of his gallery to the station corresponding to that chosen by the superior in the lodge, may perhaps not be capable of being decided to a certainty without experiment. If a bell be necessary, it may be convenient to have one for every tube; and the wire, by running in the tube as in a sheath, will be preserved from accidents.**

The other set of conversation-tubes is to enable an inspector

---

* About the size of a *pea shooter*, a plaything used by children for blowing peas, will probably be sufficient.

** The power possessed by metallic tubes of conveying the slightest whispers to an almost indefinite distance, can be no secret to such readers as have seen any of the exhibitions of speaking figures, whose properties depend upon this principle.

Many a reader may also have seen Mr. Merlin's ingenious contrivance of written tablets of orders, for masters above to servants below, an index pointing to a tablet in the superior room, giving motion to an index pointing to a duplicate tablet in the inferior room, upon the principle of the drawing machine called a *pantograph*. The conversation-tubes above mentioned, might perhaps supply the place of those order-tablets, and, if it all, with very considerable advantage. The intercourse by the tablets is *limited* to the few orders they can be made to hold: it is not reciprocal. The apparatus, from what I recollect of Mr. Merlin's price, would, I should suppose, be more expensive.

SELECTIONS FROM POSTSCRIPT I

in the lodge to hold converse in his own person, whenever he thinks proper, with a prisoner in any of the cells. Fixed tubes, crossing the annular well, and continued to so great a length, being plainly out of the question, the tubes for this purpose can be no other than the short ones in common use under the name *speaking-trumpets*. To an inspector stationed in the lodge, it is not indeed in every part of every cell that a prisoner with whom he may have occasion to hold converse

---

For such purposes, the tube alone, without a bell, would answer the purpose, supposing the servant to be in the room into which it opened, and not unwilling to receive the order: but for summoning him from a distant part of the house, and for putting a negative upon all pretence of not hearing, nothing, it is evident, but a bell, can serve.

The tube, as already mentioned, might serve as a sheath to inclose the bell: thus the expense of the sheaths, which are at present employed in some cases, would be saved. At the places where cranks are necessary, the tubes, that the continuity may not be broken, must be enlarged to receive them. Whether the voice would continue intelligible, as well as audible, after so many inflexions of the tube as may be necessary in some cases in common houses, is more than, without experiment, I can pretend to say. In the present case, there is but one angle, and even that, in case of necessity, might be got rid of.

Wire, by its rigidity, being liable to twist and snap, perhaps the flax of New South Wales, when that admirable commodity comes to be supplied in sufficient quantities for manufacture, might be substituted with advantage.

Under the different mouth-pieces opening into the servants' apartment, might be painted the names of the rooms to which they respectively corresponded.

Copper, by those who would not grudge the expense, would on several accounts be evidently preferable to tin. In the master's apartment, gilt mouth-pieces would form an ornamental addition to the furniture.

It is certainly an awkward circumstance, and which occasions much waste of time in families, for a servant to be obliged to go up three or four pair of stairs to receive orders which are to be executed in the kitchen from whence he came.

Since writing the above, I recollect having seen a tube employed for this purpose many years ago at Messrs. Nairne and Blunt's, mathematical instrument makers, in Cornhill, to great advantage. It reaches from the bottom of the staircase to a level with a workshop in the garret.

At Mr. Merlin's, too, I recollect having heard of an instance in which the principle is employed in a piece of mechanism set up since I was there. Discourse is carried on in whispers between two persons addressing themselves to two heads set up at the opposite ends of a long room. There must therefore be two angles made; two perpendicular tubes inserted into an horizontal one.

It is curious to think what a length of time an idea may lie, without receiving some of its most obvious as well as useful applications. For how many centuries was the art of engraving for impressions practised to inimitable perfection on small stones, without its occurring to any one to apply it to plates or types upon a large scale!

will be already visible. But to render him so, there needs but an order summoning him to the grating; which order may be delivered to him through the local subordinate, from the inspection-gallery belonging to that story of cells.

Here may be observed the first opening of that scene of clock-work regularity, which it would be so easy to establish in so compact a microcosm. Certainty, promptitude, and uniformity, are qualities that may here be displayed in the extreme. Action scarcely follows thought, quicker than execution might here be made to follow upon command.

Turn now to the good Howard's Penitentiary-town, and con-ceive a dozen task-masters and turnkeys running on every occasion from one corner of it to the other and back again (little less than ¼ of a mile) to receive some order from the governor, the prisoners their own masters all the while.

Hither come the customers to such prisoners as exercise their original trades; at stated times to bring materials and take back work, and at most times to give orders. By the conversation-tubes, converse for this as well as every other permitted purpose, is circulated instantaneously, with the utmost facility, to the greatest distance. Even the intervention of the local inspector is not necessary: a call from a speaking-trumpet brings the remotest prisoner to the front of his cell, where he may be seen by the customer, as well as heard. Under each speaking-trumpet hangs a list of the prisoners to whose cells it corresponds. The names are on separate cards, which are shifted as often as a prisoner happens to be shifted from cell to cell. As to the two lowest stories of cells, converse with them may be carried on directly from the corresponding inspection-gallery.

The lodge may serve as a common room for all the officers of the house. Of its division into male and female sides, I speak elsewhere. On the male side, the sub-governor, the chaplain, the surgeon, and perhaps another officer, such as the head schoolmaster, may have each his separate apartment, divided, however, from the rest no otherwise than by a moveable screen, not reaching to the ceiling, and leaving free passage as well round the central aperture as round the inspection-platform attached to the surrounding wall.

In this same apartment, the officers, male and female, may

take their meals in common. Room is not wanting. Why not, as well as fellows in a college? This surely would not be the least active nor least useful of all colleges. Too much of their time cannot be spent in this central station, when not wanted on immediate duty. No expedient that can help to bring them hither, or keep them here, ought to be neglected. The legitimate authority of the governor and sub-governor will here receive assistance, their arbitrary power restraint, from the presence of their associates in office. A governor, a sub-governor, will blush, if not fear, to issue any tyrannical order in presence of so many disapproving witnesses; whose opinion, tacit or expressed, will be a bridle upon his management, though without power to oppose and disturb it. Monarchy, with publicity and responsibility for its only checks: such is the best, or rather the only tolerable form of government for such an empire.

In Mr. Howard's Penitentiary-town, each officer has his house – all separate, and all out of sight and hearing of the prisoners. This latter arrangement may be the more agreeable one of the two to the servant; but which is the best adapted to the service?

The want of side windows, as in other rooms, will render it eligible at least, if not necessary, to make a provision of *air-holes* for the purpose of ventilation.

The supports to the surrounding gallery, as shown in the engraved plan, might, if made hollow, answer this intention, and save the making an apparatus of tubes on purpose. In this case, however, each support would require a horizontal tube inserted into it at right angles, which might run close and parallel to the conversation-tubes, immediately under the ceiling.

It is at the level of the ceiling that these air-tubes should discharge themselves into the lodge, and not at the level of the floor. In the latter case, they could not answer this intention without a continual blast, which in cold weather would be very troublesome. In the other way, the blast beginning above the level of the head, is directed upwards, and gives no annoyance. Health is not bought at the expense of comfort.

In giving the slope to the ceiling in manner above mentioned, I had two conveniences in view: ventilation and stowage. To ventilation, which is the principal object, a rectilinear slope in this case is more favourable, not only than a horizontal ceiling, but even than a coved ceiling or dome. Both would have left a space untraversed by the current: in the one case, the space would have been angular; in the other, there would still have remained some space for stagnant air, though lessened by the abrasion of the angle.

The reduction of the height of the ceiling at this part leaves a quantity of room, of which some use may be made in the way of *stowage*. From the area of the chapel, the floor must, as well as the ceiling below, have a certain degree of slope to afford the second story of cells a view of the minister. But the declivity in the ceiling begins, not under the *circumference* of that area, but much nearer the centre, viz. at the central aperture. Hence, after necessary allowance for thickness of floor and ceiling, there will remain a void space of considerable extent all round, the exact dimensions of which it is needless to particularise. Disposing the slope here and there in regular and gentle flights of steps, for the purpose of communication, in other places the thickness of 2 or 3 or 4 steps may be laid together, to receive drawers or presses.

A place still more convenient in proportion to the extent of it in the way of stowage, will be the space immediately underneath the inspector's platform in the lodge. It will serve for presses or drawers opening into the surrounding gallery.

A more considerable space runs from behind the two superior galleries, under the steps of the chapel-galleries to which they are respectively attached. Tools and materials of work, of which the bulk is not very considerable, will find very convenient receptacles in these several places, where they will be in readiness to be delivered out and received back, by being handed over the annular well, to the prisoners in their cells.

As to the mode of *warming* the lodge, it will be considered in the section so entitled.*

---

* How to reconcile the use of the lodge as a dining-room with the purity of air necessary to the reception of company in the chapel? By making the Saturday's dinner the last meal, dedicating to ventilation the whole interval between that period and the commencement of divine service in the ensuing day.

A FRAGMENT

ON

ONTOLOGY

CONTENTS

ONTOLOGY.

.

INTRODUCTION.

THE most general, that is, the most extensive propositions belonging to physics, to *somatology*, the only branch of physics that comes under the cognisance of sense, are considered as forming a separate branch of art and science, under the very uncharacteristic name of mathematics.

The most general and extensive propositions belonging to physics, in the largest sense of the word, including Somatology* and Psychology** taken together, have been considered as forming, in like manner, a separate discipline, to which the name of Ontology has been assigned.

The field of Ontology, or as it may otherwise be termed, the field of supremely abstract entities is a yet untrodden labyrinth, – a wilderness never hitherto explored.

In the endeavour to bring these entities to view, and place them under the reader's eye in such sort that to each of their names, ideas as clear, correct, and complete as possible, may by every reader who will take the trouble, be annexed and remain attached, the following is the course that will be pursued.

Those of which the conception is most simple, will all along

---

* Somatology, the science that belongs to bodies.

** Psychology, the science that belongs to mind.

precede those of which the conception is less simple; in other words, those words to the understanding of which, neither any other word, nor the import of any other word, will be necessary, will be brought to view in the first place, and before any of those which in their import bear a necessary and more or less explicit or implied reference to the ideas attached to this or that other word.

CHAPTER I.
CLASSIFICATION OF ENTITIES.

SECTION I.
Division of Entities.

An entity is a denomination in the import of which every subject matter of discourse, for the designation of which the grammatical part of speech called a noun-substantive is employed, may be comprised.

Entities may be distinguished into *perceptible* and *inferential*.

An entity, whether perceptible or inferential, is either real or fictitious.

SECTION II.
Of Perceptible Entities.

A *perceptible* entity is every entity the existence of which is made know to human beings by the immediate testimony of their senses, without reasoning, *i.e.* without reflection. A perceptible real entity is, in one word, a body.*

The name *body* is the name of the genus generalissimum of that class of real entities. Under this genus generalissimum, a system of divisions which has for its limit the aggregate of all distinguishable individual bodies, may be pursued through as many stages as are found conducive to the purposes of discourse, at any such stage, and at any number of such stages,

---

* The name *substance* has, by the logicians of former times, been used to comprise perceptible and inferential real entities: Souls, God, Angels, Devils, have been designated by them by the appellation *substance*.

the mode of division may be bifurcate* and exhaustive, *i.e.* all-comprehensive.

The division according to which bodies are spoken of as subjects of one or other of the three physical kingdoms, viz. animal, vegetable, and mineral, is a *trifurcate* division. By substituting to this one stage of division, two stages, each of them bifurcate, the division may be rendered, or rather shown to be, exhaustive; as thus: –

A body is either endued with life, or not endued with life.

A body endued with life, is either endued with sensitive life, or with life not sensitive.

A body endued with sensitive life, is an animal; a body endued with a life not sensitive, is a vegetable; a body not endued with life, is a mineral.

SECTION III.
Of Inferential Entities.

An *inferential* entity, is an entity which, in these times at least, is not made known to human beings in general, by the testimony of sense, but of the existence of which the persuasion is produced by reflection – is inferred from a chain of reasoning.

An inferential entity is either, 1. Human; or 2. Super-human.

1. A human inferential entity, is the soul considered as existing in a state of separation from the body.

Of a human soul, existing in a state of separation from the body, no man living will, it is believed, be found ready to aver himself to have had perception of any individual example; or, at any rate, no man who, upon due and apposite interrogation would be able to obtain credence.

Considered as existing and visiting any part of our earth in a state of separation from the body, a human soul would be a ghost: and, at this time of day, *custom* scarcely does, *fashion* certainly does not command us to believe in ghosts.

---

* The use of the exhaustive mode of division, as contradistinguished from that which is not exhaustive, *i.e.* all-comprehensive, is to show, that your conception and comprehension of the subject, in so far as the particulars comprehended in it are in view, is complete.

Of this description of beings, the reality not being, in any instance, attested by *perception,* cannot therefore be considered any otherwise than as a matter of *inference.**

2. A superhuman entity is either supreme or subordinate.

The supreme, superhuman, inferential entity is God: sanctioned by revelation; sanctioned by the religion of Jesus as delivered by the apostle Paul, is the proposition that no man hath seen God at any time. If this proposition be correct, God not being consistently with the imperfection of the human senses capable of being referred to the class of perceptible real entities, cannot, in consequence of the imperfection under which human reason labours, cannot, any more than the soul of man considered as existing in a separate state, be referred by it to any other class than that of inferential real entities as above described.**

A subordinate superhuman entity is either *good* or *bad.* A good subordinate superhuman inferential entity is an angel; a bad subordinate superhuman inferential entity is a devil.

By the learner as well as by the teacher of logic, all these subjects of Ontology may, without much detriment, it is believed, to any other useful art, or any other useful science, be left in the places in which they are found.

SECTION IV.
Of Real Entities.

A *real* entity is an entity to which, on the occasion and for the purpose of discourse, existence is really meant to be ascribed.

---

* Should there be any person in whose view the soul of man, considered in a state of separation from the body, should present itself as not capable of being, with propriety, aggregated to the class of real entities, to every such person, the class to which it belongs would naturally be that of fictitious entities; in which case it would probably be considered as being that whole, of which so many other psychical entities, none of which have ever been considered any otherwise than fictitious, such as the understanding, and the will, the perceptive faculty, the memory, and the imagination, are so many parts.

** Should there be any person who, incapable of drawing those influences by which the Creator and Preserver of all other entities, is referred to the class of real ones, should refuse to him a place in that class, the class to which such person would find himself, in a manner, compelled to refer that invisible and mysterious being would be, not as in the case of the human soul to that of fictitious entities, but that of non-entities.

Under the head of perceptible real entities may be placed, without difficulty, individual perceptions of all sorts:* the impressions produced in groups by the application of sensible objects to the organs of sense: the ideas brought to view by the recollection of those same objects; the new ideas produced under the influence of the imagination, by the decomposition and recomposition of those groups; – to none of these can the character, the denomination, of real entities be refused.

Faculties, powers of the mind, dispositions: all these are unreal; all these are but so many fictitious entities. When a view of them comes to be given, it will be seen how perfectly distinguishable, among physical entities, are those which are recognised in the character of real, from those which are here referred to the class of fictitious entities.

To some it may seem matter of doubt whether, to a perception of any kind, the appellation of a real entity can, with propriety, be applied.

Certain it is that it cannot, if either *solidity* or *permanence* be regarded as a quality belonging to the essence of reality.

But in neither of these instances can, it is believed, any sufficient or just reason be assigned, why the field of reality should be regarded as confined within the limits which, on that supposition, would be applied to it.

Whatsoever title an object belonging to the class of bodies may be considered as possessing to the attribute of reality, i.e. of existence, every object belonging to the class of *perceptions* will be found to possess, in still higher degree, a title established by more immediate evidence: it is only by the evidence afforded by perceptions that the reality of a body of any kind can be established.

Of *Ideas,* our perception is still more direct and immediate than that which we have of corporeal substances: of their existence our persuasion is more necessary and irresistible than that which we have of the existence of corporeal substances.

Speaking of Entities, ideas might perhaps accordingly be spoken of as the *sole perceptible ones*, substances, those of the

---

* Pathematic, *Apathematic*, to one or other of these denominations may all imaginable sorts of perceptions be referred. Pathematic, viz. such as either themselves consist of or are accompanied by pleasure or pain; *Apathematic,* such as have not any such accompaniment in any shape.

corporeal class, being, with reference, and in contradistinction to them, no other than *inferential* ones.

But if substances themselves be the subject of the division, and for the designation of the two branches of the division the words perceptible and inferential be employed, it is to corporeal substances that the characteristic and differential attribute, perceptible, cannot but be applied: the term inferential being thereupon employed for the designation of incorporeal ones.

The more correct and complete the consideration bestowed, the more clearly will it be perceived, that from the existence of perceptions, viz. of sensible ones, the inference whereby the existence of corporeal entities, viz. the bodies from which those perceptions are respectively derived, is much stronger, more necessary, and more irresistible, than the inference whereby the existence of incorporeal entities is inferred from the existence of perceptible entities, alias *corporeal* substances, alias bodies.

Suppose the non-existence of corporeal substances, of any hard corporeal substance that stands opposite to you, make this supposition, and as soon as you have made it, act upon it, pain, the perception of pain, will at once bear witness against you; and that by your punishment, your condign punishment. Suppose the non-existence of any inferential incorporeal substances, of any one of them, or of all of them, and the supposition made, act upon it accordingly, – be the supposition conformable or not conformable to the truth of the case, at any rate no such immediate counter-evidence, no such immediate punishment will follow.*

---

* In the works of the authors who now (anno 1813) are in vogue, not a few are the notions of which the appearance will, at this time of day, be apt to excite a sensation of surprise in an unexperienced, and one day perhaps, even in an experienced, mind.

Of this number are – 1. The denial of the existence of bodies. 2. The denial of the existence of general or abstract ideas.

Of these kindred paradoxes, – for such, in some sort, they will be found to be, – who were the first persons by whom they were respectively broached, is more than I recollect, if so it be that I ever knew; nor, supposing it attainable, would the trouble of the search be paid for by the value of the thing found.

Of those by whom the notion of the non-existence of matter, including the several bodies that present themselves to our senses, is maintained, Bishop Berkeley, if not the first in point of time, is, at any rate, the most illustrious partisan.

SECTION V.
Of Fictitious Entities.

A *fictitious* entity is an entity to which, though by the grammatical form of the discourse employed in speaking of it, existence by ascribed, yet in truth and reality existence is not meant to be ascribed.

Every noun-substantive which is not the name of a real entity, perceptible or inferential, is the name of a fictitious entity.

Every fictitious entity bears some relation to some real entity, and can no otherwise be understood than in so far as that relation is perceived, – a conception of that relation is obtained.

Reckoning from the real entity to which it bears relation, a fictitious entity may be styled a fictitious entity of the first remove, a fictitious entity of the second remove, and so on.

A fictitious entity of the first remove is a fictitious entity, a conception of which may be obtained by the consideration of the relation borne by it to a real entity, without need of considering the relation borne by it to any other fictitious entity.

A fictitious entity of the second remove is a fictitious entity, for obtaining a conception of which it is necessary to take into consideration some fictitious entity of the first remove.

Considered at any two contiguous points of time, every real entity is either in motion or at rest.

Now, when a real entity is said to be at rest, it is said to be so with reference to some other particular real entity or aggregate of real entities; for so far as any part of the system of the universe is perceived by us we at all times perceive it not to be at rest. Such, at least, is the case not only with the bodies called planets, but with one or more of the bodies called fixed stars; and, by analogy, we infer this to be the case with all the rest.

This premised, considered with reference to any two contiguous points of time past, every perceptible real entity was, during that time, either in motion or not in motion; if not in motion, it was at rest.

Here, then, we have two correspondent and opposite fictitious entities of the first remove, viz. a motion and a rest.

A motion is a mode of speech commonly employed; a rest is a mode of speech not so commonly employed.

To be spoken of at all, every fictitious entity must be spoken of as if it were real. This, it will be seen, is the case with the above-mentioned pair of fictitious entities of the first remove.

A body is said to be in motion. This, taken in the literal sense, is as much as to say, here is a larger body, called a motion; *in* this larger body, the other body, namely, the really existing body, is contained.

So in regard to rest. To say this body is at rest is as much as to say, here is a body, and it will naturally be supposed a fixed body, and here is another body, meaning the real existing body, which is *at* that first-mentioned body, *i.e.* attached to it, as if the fictitious body were a stake, and the real body a beast tied to it.

An instance of fictitious entity of the second remove is a quality. There are qualities that are qualities of real entities; there are qualities that are qualities of the above-mentioned fictitious entities of the first remove. For example, of motion, rectilinearity, curvilinearity, slowness, quickness, and so on.

SECTION VI.
Uses of this distinction between names of Real and names of Fictitious Entities.

These uses are, 1. Attaching, in the only way in which they can be attached, clear ideas to the several all-comprehensive and leading terms in question. 2. Obviating and excluding the multitudinous errors and disputes of which the want of such clear ideas has been the source: disputes which, in many instances, have not terminated in words, but through words have produced antipathy, and through antipathy war with all its miseries.

Fictitious entity says some one, – of such a locution where can be the sense or use? By the word *entity* cannot but be represented something that has existence, – apply to the same subject the adjunct *fictitious*, the effect is to give instruction that it has not any existence. This, then, is a contradiction in terms, a species of locution from which, in proportion as it has any employment, confusion, and that alone, cannot but be the effect.

Entities are either real or fictitious, what can that mean? What but that of entities there are two species or sorts: viz. one which is itself, and another which is neither itself nor anything else? Instead of fictitious entity, or as synonymous with fictitious entity, why not here say, *nonentity?*

Answer. – Altogether inevitable will this seeming contradiction be found. The root of it is in the nature of language: that instrument without which, though of itself it be nothing, nothing can be said, and scarcely can anything be done.

Of the nature of that instrument, of the various forms under which it has been seen to present itself among different tribes of men, of the indispensable parts (*i.e.* parts of speech) which may be seen to belong to it under every one of those forms, actual or possible, of the qualities desirable on the part of the collection of signs of which, under all these several forms, it is composed: – under all these several heads, sketches will be endeavoured to be given in another place.

All this while, antecedently to the stage at which these topics will present themselves, use is however making, as it could not but be made, of this same instrument. At that future stage, it will not only be the *instrument*, but the *subject* also of inquiry: at present and until then, employing it in the character of an instrument, we must be content to take it in hand, and make use of it, in the state in which we find it.

In like manner, the several operations, which by the help of language, and under the direction of logic, are performed by human minds upon language and thereby upon minds: such as distinction, division, definition, and the several other modes of exposition, including those of methodization, must be performed at and from the very outset of a work on logic, antecedently to the stage at which the task of examining into their nature and origination will be entered upon and come to be performed.

To language, then – to language alone – it is, that fictitious entities owe their existence – their impossible, yet indispensable, existence.*

---

* The division of entities into real and fictitious, is more properly the division of names into *names* of real and *names* of fictitious entities.

In language the words which present themselves, and are employed in the character of *names*, are, some of them, names of real entities, – others, names of fictitious entities; and to one or other of these classes may all words which are employed in the character of *names* be referred.

What will, moreover, be seen, is, that the fiction – the mode of representation by which the fictitious entities thus created, in so far as fictitious entities can be created, are dressed up in the garb, and placed upon the level, of real ones, is a contrivance but for which language, or, at any rate, language in any form superior to that of the language of the brute creation, could not have existence.

And now, perhaps, may be seen the difference between a *fictitious entity* and a *non-entity*: or, to speak more strictly, the difference between the import of the two words – a difference such, that when, with propriety and use, the one is, the other cannot be employed.

In the house designated by such a number, (naming it) in such a street, in such a town, lives a being called the Devil, having a head, body, and limbs, like a man's – horns like a goat's – wings like a bat's, and a tail like a monkey's: – Suppose this assertion made, the observation naturally might be, that the Devil, as thus described, is a non-entity. The averment made of it is, that an object of that description really exists. Of that averment, if seriously made, the object or end in view cannot but be to produce in the minds to which communication is thus made, a serious persuasion of the existence of an object conformable to the description thus expressed.

Thus much concerning a non-entity. Very different is the notion here meant to be presented by the term fictitious entity.

By this term is here meant to be designated one of those sorts of objects, which in every language must, for the purpose of discourse, be spoken of as existing, – be spoken of in the like manner as those objects which really have existence, and to which existence is seriously meant to be ascribed, are spoken of; but without any such danger as that of producing any such persuasion as that of their possessing, each for itself, any separate, or strictly speaking, any real existence.

Take, for instances, the words motion, relation, faculty, power, and the like.

Real entities being the objects for the designation of which, in the first place, at the earliest stage of human intercourse, and in virtue of the most urgent necessity, words, in the character of names, were employed, – between the idea of a name and that of the reality of the object to which it was applied, an association being thus formed, from a connexion thus intimate, sprung a very natural propensity, viz. that of attributing reality to every object thus designated; – in a word, of ascribing reality to the objects designated by words, which, upon due examination, would be found to be nothing but so many names of so many fictitious entities.

To distinguish them from those fictitious entities, which, so long as language is in use among human beings, never can be spared, fabulous may be the name employed for the designation of the other class of *unreal* entities.

Of fictitious entities, whatsoever is predicated is not, consistently with strict truth, predicated (it then appears) of anything but their respective names.

But forasmuch as by reason of its length and compoundedness, the use of the compound denomination, *name of a fictitious entity*, would frequently be found attended with inconvenience; for the avoidance of this inconvenience, instead of this long denomination, the less long, though, unhappily, still compound denomination, fictitious entity, will commonly, after the above warning, be employed.

Of nothing that has place, or passes, in our minds can we give any account, any otherwise than by speaking of it as if it were a portion of space, with portions of matter, some of them at rest, others moving in it. Of nothing, therefore, that has place, or passes in our mind, can we speak, or so much as think, otherwise than in the way of *fiction*. To this word fiction we must not attach either those sentiments of pleasure, or those sentiments of displeasure, which, with so much propriety, attach themselves to it on the occasion in which it is most commonly in use. Very different in respect of purpose and necessity, very different is this logical species of fiction from the poetical and political; – very different the fiction of the Logician from the fictions of poets, priests, and lawyers.

For their object and effect, the fictions with which the Logician is conversant, without having been the author of them, have had neither more nor less than the carrying on of human converse; such communication and interchange of thought as is capable of having place between man and man. The fictions of the poet, whether in his character of historic fabulist or dramatic fabulist, putting or not putting the words of his discourse in metrical form, are pure of insincerity, and, neither for their object nor for their effect have anything but to amuse, unless it be in some cases to excite to action – to action in this or that particular direction for this or that particular purpose. By the priest and the lawyer, in whatsoever shape fiction has been employed, it has had for its object or effect, or both, to deceive, and, by deception, to govern, and, by governing, to promote the interest, real or supposed, of the party addressing, at the expense of the party addressed. In the mind of all, fiction, in the logical sense, has been the coin of necessity; – in that of poets of amusement – in that of the priest and the lawyer of mischievous immorality in the shape of mischievous ambition, – and too often both priest and lawyer have framed or made in part this instrument.

CHAPTER II.
FICTITIOUS ENTITIES CLASSIFIED.

SECTION I.
Names of Physical Fictitious Entities.

To this class belong all those entities which will be found included in Aristotle's list – included in his *Ten Predicaments*, the first excepted.

In the order in which he has placed and considered them, they stand as follows: – 1. Substance. 2. Quantity. 3. Quality. 4. Relation. 5. Places. 6. Time. 7. Situation. 8. Possession. 9. Action. 10. Passion or Suffering.

From this list of Aristotle's – the list of names of physical entities will, as here presented, be found to be in a considerable degree different; viz. in the first place, in respect of the particulars of which it is composed: in the next place, in respect of the order in which they are brought to view. Of these differences the grounds will successively be brought to view as they arise.

1. Quantity. – Quantity cannot exist without some substance of which it is the quantity. Of substance, no species, no individual can exist, without existing in some certain quantity.

2. Quality. – Quality cannot exist without some substance of which it is the quality. Of substance, no species can exist without being of some quality; of a multitude of qualities, of which the number is, in every instance, indeterminate, capable of receiving increase, and that to an indefinite degree, according to the purposes for which, and the occasions on which, the several substances of which they are qualities, may come to be considered.

3. Place. – Of place, the notion cannot be entertained without the notion of some substance considered as *placed*, or capable of existing, or, as we say, being *placed* in it.

Place may be considered as *absolute* or relative. Supposing but one substance in existence, that substance would be in some place, – that place would be absolute place – relative place there could be none. Suppose two substances, – then, in addition to its own absolute place, each substance would have a *relative* place, – a place constituted by the position occupied by it in relation to the other.

Of no individual substance is any notion commonly entertained without some notion of a place – a relative place as being occupied by it.

The place considered as occupied by an individual substance is different, according to the purpose for which, and the occasion on which, the substance is taken into consideration.

Expressive of the notion of place, in their original, physical, archetypal signification, are the several words termed prepositions of place and adverbs of place: These are –

In; on, or upon; under; at; above; below; round; around; out – out of; from above; from under; from.

4. Time. – Time is, as it were, on an ulterior and double account, a fictitious entity, – its denominations so many names of fictitious entities.

Compared with substance, and, in particular, with body, place is, as hath been seen, a fictitious entity. Without some body *placed* in it, or considered as being capable of being placed in it, place would have no existence, or what, with reference to use, would amount to the same thing, there would be no purpose for which, – no occasion on which, it could be considered as having existence.

But if, putting substance out of consideration, place be a fiction, time is, so to speak, a still more fictitious fiction, having nothing more substantial to lean upon than the fiction of place.

To be capable of being spoken of, time itself must be, cannot but be, spoken of as a modification of space. Witness the prepositions *in* and *at: in* such a portion of time – *at* such a portion of time; *in* an hour, – *at* 12 o' clock; *in* such a year, month, day, *at* such an hour, *at* so many seconds after such a minute in such an hour.

Witness, again, the common expressions – a short time, a long time, a space of time.

By a line it is that every portion of time, every particular time, is conceived, represented, and spoken of; – by a line, *i.e.* a body, of which the length alone, without breadth or depth, is considered.

5. Motion. 6. Rest. 7. Action. 8. Passion.

At every step the subject of consideration becomes more and more complicated.

Rest is the absence or negation of motion. Every body is either *in* motion or at rest. Here *place*, i.e. *relative space*, is still the archetype. Motion is a thing, an imaginary, an involuntarily imagined substance, *in* which the body is conceived as being placed. Rest a like body, *at* which the real body is considered as being placed.

In the idea of *motion* that of *time* is, moreover, involved, and again, that of *place*, as being that in which the idea of time is, by the like necessity, involved.

In motion a body cannot have been but it must have been in two different places, at or in two different, which is as much as to say, in two successive portions of time.

For the space of time in question, i.e. for a portion of time composed of those same portions which were operative in the case of motion, the body has been at rest, in so far as in all that space or length of time it has not changed its place with reference to any others.

Taken in the aggregate, in so far as can be concluded, either from observation or from analogy in the way of inference, no body whatsoever is, or ever has been, or ever will be, absolutely in a state of rest, *i.e.* without being in motion with reference to some other body or bodies.

The earth which we inhabit is not at rest. The sun himself about which she moves is not at rest. The stars called *fixed*, being but so many suns, are themselves no more at rest than is he.

Considered as a *whole*, the parts of our earth are, as far as appears, with reference to one another, the greater part of them always at rest, – others, especially those near the surface, many of them occasionally *in* motion: and so in regard to the several separate bodies, consisting of such portions of the matter of which the earth is composed, as are detached and separate from one another, each of them having between itself and every other, with the exception of the base on which it stands, and upon which, by the principle of attraction under the several forms under which it operates, it is kept at that place, certain portions of intervening space.

Of such of them as are in a state of solidity, rest, relative rest, rest with relation to each other, in so far as they are in that state, is the naturally constant state. *In* motion they are not *put* but by some supervening accident operating from without. Of such of them as are in a state of fluidity, liquidity and gaseosity included, motion, relative motion is, in every instance, a natural state, exemplified to a greater or lesser extent, depending partly on the particular qualities of the several fluids, partly upon the accidents *ab extra* to which, individually taken, they happen to have been exposed.

In addition to the idea of motion, in the ideas of *action* and *passion*, the idea of causation or causality is involved. The body F is in motion; – of such motion, what is the cause? *Answer*: The action of another body, the body S, which, by the influence or correspondent power which it possesses becomes productive of that effect.

In themselves the two fictitious entities, Action and Passion, are not only correspondent, but inseparable. No action without passion – no passion without action; – no action on the one part without passion on the other.

In the case of action, and thereupon on the part of one of two bodies, motion, perceptible motion, – on the part of the other body, is relative motion, in every instance a never failing consequence? To judge from analogy, the probability seems to be in the affirmative.*

In so far as on the part of one of the two alone, any motion is perceptible, on the part of the other, no motion being perceptible, the one of which the motion is perceptible, is most commonly spoken of as *the agent*, the other as the *patient:* a state of motion is the state in which the former is said to be *in*, a state of passion the state in which the other is said to be *in*.

9. Relation. – Under this head, such is its amplitude, several of the others seem totally or partially to be included – viz. 1. Quantity, all quantities bear some relation or other to each other. 2. Quality.

SECTION II.
Absolute Fictitious Entities of the first Order.
1. Matter. 2. Form. 3. Quantity. 4. Space.

No substance can exist but it must be itself *matter;* be of a certain determinate *form;* be or exist in a certain determinate *quantity;* and, were there but one substance in existence, all these three attributes would belong to it.

Matter, at first sight, may naturally enough be considered as exactly synonymous to the word *substance*. It may undoubtedly be with propriety employed instead of substance on many of the occasions on which the word substance may, with equal propriety, be employed.

But there are occasions on which, while substance may, matter cannot, with propriety be employed.

By the word *substance,* substances incorporeal, as well as corporeal, are wont to be designated; the word matter is wont to be employed to designate corporeal to the exclusion of incorporeal substances.

On the other hand, neither are occasions wanting in which, while the word *matter* may, the word substance *cannot,* with propriety be employed.

---

* 1. The earth and a projected stone.
  2. A larger and a lesser magnet.
  3. Liquids and gasses.

Matter is wont to be employed in contradistinction to *form*; and that, on occasions in which the word *substance* cannot, with propriety, be employed. Thus, in considering substance, any individual substance, consideration may be had of its matter, without any consideration had of its *form;* and so *vice versa* of its *form* without its matter.

Thus it is, that, taken in that sense which is peculiar to it, the idea attached to the word *matter* cannot, by means of that word, be brought to view without bringing to view along with it, the idea of another *entity* called form; and this is the reason why, along with *form,* it has been considered as composing a group of entities distinct from the sort of entity, for the designation of which the word substance has been employed.

The word *substance* is the name of a class of real entities of, the only class which has in it any corporeal entities.

The word *matter* is but the name of a class of fictitious entities, springing out of the sort of real entity distinguished by the word *substance.*

And so it is in regard to the word *form.*

The ideas respectively designated by these corresponding words are fractional results, produced from the decomposition of the word *substance.*

Every real physical entity, every corporeal substance, every sort of body has its matter and form; and this its matter, and this its form are entities totally different from each other.

These names of entities possess, both of them, the characteristic properties of fictitious entities. It is by means of propositions designative of place, and, by that means, of a fictitious material image, that their images are connected with the name of the real entity substance.

In that substance exists such and such matter; behold the matter of that substance; behold all this matter from that substance. Here substance is a receptacle; matter a fictitious entity, spoken of in one of these occasions as if it were a real entity contained within that receptacle; in the others as one that had proceeded from it.

Behold the *form* in which that substance presents itself; behold the form, the figure, the shape, the configuration *of* that substance.

Figure, configuration, shape, in these several words may be seen so many synonyms, or almost synonyms, to the word *form*.

Quantity has been distinguished into *continuous* and *discrete*.

Discrete quantity (it is commonly said) is number; it should rather be said is *composed of numbers:* viz. of numbers more than one, of separate entities.

It is only by means of discrete quantity, *i.e.* number, that continuous quantity can be measured by the mind; that any precise idea of any particular quantity can be formed.

To form an idea of any continuous quantity, *i.e.* of a body as existing in a certain quantity, one of two courses must be taken or conceived to be taken in relation to it. It must be divided, or conceived to be divided, into parts, *i.e.* into a determinate number of parts, or together with other similar bodies made up into a new, and artificial, and compounded whole.

To divide a body, or conceive a body to be divided into parts, it suffices not to divide it, or conceive it divided, into its constituent bodies, into any such smaller bodies as are contained in it. Either the entire body itself, or its parts respectively, must, by the mind, be conceived to be divided into its several *dimensions*.

Be the body what it may, not being boundless, it cannot but have some *bound* or *bounds*; if one, it is a surface; these *bounds,* if there be more than one, are surfaces: these surfaces again, not being boundless, have their bounds, – these bounds are lines.

The only bodies that have each of them but one uniform surface are spheres.

Bodies are real entities. Surfaces and lines are but fictitious entities. A surface without depth, a line without thickness, was never seen by any man; no; nor can any conception be seriously formed of its existence.

Space is the negation or absence of body.

Of any determinate individual portion of space, as clear an idea is capable of being formed as of any body, or of any portion of any body; and besides, being equally determinate as that of body, the idea of space is much more simple.

To *space* it is difficult either to ascribe or to deny *existence,* without a contradiction in terms; to consider it as nothing, or as distinct from nothing.

Of body, – that is of all bodies whatsoever, – the annihilation may be conceived without difficulty. Why? Because, in whatsoever place, – that is, within whatsoever portion of space, within whatsoever receptacle, composed of mere space, any body is, at any given time conceived to be, it may thenceforward be conceived to be removed from that place, and so successively from any and every other portion of space.

Of space, – that is, of all portions of space whatever, indeed of so much as any one portion of space, the annihilation cannot easily be conceived. Why? Because in *mere* space there is nothing to remove; nothing that can be conceived capable of being removed. In so far as matter is annihilated, there is less matter than there was before. But, suppose space to be annihilated; is there less space than there was before?

Hence, taken in the aggregate, no bounds, no limits can be assigned to space; so neither can any *form* or any *quantity*. It cannot be removed; it cannot be moved; for there is nothing of it or in it to remove; there is no place to which it can be removed.

So much for *space* taken in the *aggregate*; but take this or that individual portion of space, the properties of it are very different. Conceive it, as in innumerable instances it really is, enclosed in bodies, immediately it is, and unavoidably, you conceive it to be endowed with many of the properties of bodies. Of limits it is susceptible, as body is; in point of fact it has limits; and, having these limits, it thereby has not only form but quantity. It not only has limits as truly as body has limits, but it has *the same limits*.

Having limits, it thereby has form, quantity, and even motion: along with the terraqueous globe, – *i.e.* with the whole matter of it, – all the portions of space enclosed in that matter describe round the sun, and with the sun, their continually repeated and ever varied round.

Substance being a real physical entity, – perceptions real psychical entities, – matter, form, quantity, and so on, so many fictitious entities, both descriptions being in part applicable to space, neither of them applicable entirely, – space may be regarded and spoken of as a *semi-real entity*.

SECTION III.
Absolute Fictitious Entities of the second Order.
1. Quality. 2. Modification.

Matter, Form, Quantity, – all these are susceptible of Quality. Matter, every portion of it, is capable of having its qualities, independently of those of its form and those of its quantity.

A body is said to be of such a *quality;* such or such a quality is said to be *in* it, *resident, inherent,* in it. The matter, the form, the quantity of this body, – in any one of these fictitious entities may this secondary fictitious entity be said to be resident, to be inherent.

Between quantity and quality, a sort of reciprocation, a sort of reciprocal intercommunion may be observed to have place. As we have the *quality* of a quantity – two qualities, for instance, vastness, minuteness, &c., – so has a quality its quantities.

The *quantity* of a *quality* is termed a degree.

The term *modification* is nearly synonymous to the term quality.

Of modification it seems scarcely proper to speak, as constituting or being a fictitious entity different and distinct from *quality*: the difference between them is rather of a grammatical than of a logical nature. Yet, of the cases in which the word quality may be employed, there are some in which the word *modification* can scarcely, without impropriety, be employed. We may speak of a modification of this or that body, or of the matter, form, or quantity, as well as of a quality *of* that same body; but we can scarcely, without impropriety, speak of a modification as being a thing *resident* or *inherent* in that same body.

By the word quality it is, that are expressed all particulars whereby the condition of the body, or other object in question, is rendered similar or dissimilar – in the first place, to that of itself at different times, in the next place, to that of other bodies or objects, whether at a different, or at the same time.

Goodness and *badness,* of all qualities experienced or imaginable, these are the very first that would present themselves to notice, these are the very first that would obtain names. Interest *i.e.* desire of pleasure and of exemption from pain, being, in some shape or other, the source of every thought, as well as the cause of every action (and, in particular, amongst others of every action by which names are employed in the designation of persons and of things, – names plainly and immediately expressive of the two opposite modes of relation, in which those objects would be continually bearing relation to each man's interest, as above explained) would be among the very earliest to which the faculty of discourse would give existence.

Synonyms, or quasi synonyms to quality, – in this character may be mentioned: – 1. Nature; 2. Sort; 3. Kind; 4. Mode; 5. Complexion; 6. Description; 7. Character; 8. Shape; viz. in a sense somewhat less extensive than that in which it is, as above, synonymous with Form.

SECTION IV.
Fictitious Entities connected with Relation, enumerated.

No two entities of any kind can present themselves simultaneously to the mind; no, nor can so much as the same object present itself at different times, without presenting the idea of *Relation.* For relation is a fictitious entity, which is produced, and has place, as often as the mind, having perception of any one object, obtains, at the same, or at any immediately succeeding instant, perception of any other object, or even of that same object, if the perception be accompanied with the perception of its being the same; *Diversity* is, in the one case, the name of the relation, *Identity* in the other case. But, as identity is but the negation of diversity, thence if, on no occasion, diversity had ever been, neither, on any occasion, would any such idea as that of identity have come into existence.

Whatsoever two entities, real or fictitious, come to receive names, and thus to receive their nominal existence, *Relation* would be the third; for, between the two, they being, by the supposition, different, and both of them actual objects of perception, the relation of difference or diversity would also become an object of perception, and in the character of a fictitious entity, a production of the acts of abstraction and denomination, acquire its nominal existence.

Next, after *matter* and *form,* the fictitious-entity relation, or the class of fictitious entities called *Relations,* might, therefore, have been brought to view. But not only between matter and form, but also between the one and the other respectively, and the fictitious entities designated by the words quantity, space, and quality, so close seemed the connexion as not to be, without sensible inconvenience, broken by the interposition of any other.

Once introduced upon the carpet, the fictitious entity called relation swells into an extent such as to swallow up all the others. Every other fictitious entity is seen to be but a mode of this.

The most extensive, and, in its conception, simple of all relations, *i.e.* of all modes or modifications of the fictitious entity, denominated *relation,* is that of *place,* with its submodifications.

Next to that in the order of simplicity comes the modification of *time,* with its submodifications.

Next to them come successively the relations designated by the several words, motion, rest, action, passion. Subalternation, viz. logical subalternation, opposition, and connexion, or the relation between cause and effect.

Existence, with its several modifications, or correspondent fictitious entities; non-existence, futurity, actuality, potentiality, necessity, possibility, and impossibility will, with most convenience, close the rear. Though still more extensive than even relation, they could not be brought to view before it, being applicable to all other relations, – to relations of all sorts, and in a word, to entities, whether fictitious or real, of all sorts, – no complete, or so much as correct view of their nature and character could be given, till these less extensive ones had been brought to view.

SECTION V.
*Simple Fictitious Entities connected
with Relation.*

Place. – Of the species of relation designated by the word *place,* the most perfect conception may be easily formed by taking into the account the species of relation designated by the word *time*.

Necessary altogether is the relation which the species of fictitious entity called *place* has, on the one hand, to the fictitious entity called *body,* on the other hand, to the fictitious entity called *space.*

Space may be distinguished into *absolute* and *relative.* To absolute space there are no conceivable bounds; to relative space, *i.e.* to portions of space separated from one or other by bodies, there *are,* in every instance, bounds, and those determinate ones.

As to the word *place,* whether it be considered as the name of a real entity or as the name of a fictitious entity, would be a question of words, barely worth explanation, and not at all worth debate.

Considered as a modification of space, it would, like *that,* stand upon the footing of the name of a real entity; considered as a species of relation, it would stand upon the footing of a fictitious entity. But in this latter case comes an objection: viz. that the relations which on that occasion are in question, are not place itself, or places themselves, but such *relations* as *belong* to place.

Be this as it may, place is a relative portion of space, considered either as actually occupied, or as capable of being occupied, by some real entity of the class of bodies.

Portions of the earth's surface are considered and denominated each of them a place; but in this case, the term *place* is used in the *physical* and *geographical* sense of the word, not in an *ontological* sense.

Whether, in a *physical* sense, place be or be not the name of a fictitious entity, that in every *physical* sense it is so, seems manifest beyond dispute. Take, for example, the *place* occupied by such or such an idea in the mind, by such or such a transaction in a narrative.

Time. – Be it as it may in regard to place, that the entity designated by the word *time* is but a fictitious entity, will, it is believed, be sufficiently manifest.

Different altogether from each other are the perceptions or ideas presented by the word place and the word time. Yet as often as *time* is spoken of, it is spoken of as if it were a modification of, or the same thing as *place.*

Like place, time, or at least any given portion of time, is spoken of in the character of a receptacle, – as in such or such a place things are done, in such or such a time things are done; portions of *space* or place are long or short, great or small, – so are portions of *time*. In the same sense we say, a quantity of time or a space of time. As bodies are spoken of as going *to* or *from* such or such a *place*, so operations are spoken of as going on from and to such or such a portion of time.

But of every receptacle, all the several parts are coexistent; of any portion of *time,* no two parts, how small soever, are coexistent. Of any given portion of time, no two of the parts are coexistent; with relation to each, all are successive. In the very import of the term coexistent, the idea of unity, is implied in respect of the portion of time supposed to be occupied; in the import of the term succession, that of diversity is of necessity implied.

Motion. – That the entity designated by the word *motion* is a fictitious entity seems at least equally beyond dispute.

A body, the body in question, is *in motion*: here, unless *in motion* be considered as an abbreviated expression substituted for *in a state of motion,* as we say, *in a state of rest,* motion is a receptacle, in which the body is considered as stationed. *The motion of this body* is slow or is retrograde. Here the body is a stationary object – a station or starting-post, of or from which the motion is considered as proceeding.

Necessarily included in the idea of *motion* is the idea of place and time. A body has been in motion. – When? In what case? When having, at or in one point of time, been in any one place, at another point of time it has been in any other.

Of any and every corporeal real entity, a similitude is capable of being exhibited as well in the form of a body, for instance a model, as in the form of a surface, – as in painting, or drawing, or engraving; which, in every case, is like the object represented, a stationary, permanent, and, unless by internal decay, or external force, an unchanging and unmoving object.

But by no such graphical similitude, by no picture, by no model, by no stationary object, can any motion be represented. A representation of the body as it appeared in the place occupied by it at a point of time anterior to that at which the motion commenced; a representation of the same body as it appeared in the place occupied by it at a point of time posterior to that at which the motion commenced; in these two representations, conjoined or separate, may be seen all that can be done towards the representation of motion by any permanent imitative work.

Even on the table of the mind, in imagination, in idea, in no other way can any motion be represented. There not being any real entity to represent, the entity cannot be any other than fictitious: the name employed for the purpose of representation cannot therefore be anything else than the name of a fictitious entity.

Action. – In the *idea* of action, the idea of motion is an essential ingredient. But to *actual* action, actual motion can scarcely be regarded as necessary. Action is either motion itself, or the tendency to motion. Under the term *action,* besides motion, a tendency, though so it be without actual motion, seems to be included. Held back by strings, a magnet and a bar of iron, suspended at a certain distance from each other, remain both of them without motion: cut the strings of either of them, it moves till it comes in contact with the other; but for the state of mutual action which preceded the cutting of the strings no such motion would have taken place.

Passion, Reaction. – Among all the bodies, large and small, with which we have any the slightest acquaintance, no instance, it is believed, can be found of action without passion, nor of passion without reaction. But without either of these accompaniments, a conception of action may be entertained, at any rate attention may by applied to it; but if on either of two objects, attention be capable of being bestowed without being bestowed upon the other, the separate lot of attention thus bestowed affords sufficient foundation for a separate name.

Here, then, are two more fictitious entities most nearly related and intimately connected with the fictitious entities action and motion, having all of them, for their common archetype, the same image or set of images: viz. that of a nutshell and nut, a starting-post and a goal; the representation of which is performed by the prepositions *in, of, from,* &c., employed in connexion with their respective names.

SECTION VI.

Fictitious Entities considered and denominated in respect
of their concomitancy. Object, Subject, End in View.

In the idea of an object, the idea of some action, or at any rate
some motion, seems to be constantly and essentially involved.
Where the object is a corporeal entity, it is a body towards
which the body in motion moves: this body, whether perma-
nently or momentarily, stands *objected*: *i.e. cast before* that
other body which moves.

Even in the case of vision, in the instance of an object of
sight, the relation is naturally the same; the only difference is,
that in the case of vision, the moving bodies being the rays of
light, the *object,* instead of being the body *towards* which, is
the body *from* which the motion takes place.

In the picture, the tracing of which is the effect, of the terms
here in question the *object* is either on the same level with the
source of motion, or *above* it; the *subject,* as in its literal sense,
the word *subject* imports is below and under it.

In the case of human action, – a motion, real or fictitious,
considered as being produced by an exercise of the faculty of
the will, on the part of a sensitive being, – this action has, in
every instance, for its cause, the desire and expectation of some
good, *i.e.* of some pleasure or exemption from some pain, and
the entity, the good by which this desire has been produced, is
in this case, if not the only object, an object, and, indeed, the
ultimate *object,* the attainment of which is, in the performance
of the action aimed at.

Of entities thus intimately connected, it is not to be wondered
at, if the conceptions formed, and the names bestowed in
consequence, should frequently be indistinct.

In the designation of the same entity, in the designation of
which the word *subject* is employed, the word *object* is at other
times employed: and so also in the designation of the same
entity in the designation of which the words *end in view* are
employed, the word *object* is frequently also employed.

If in a case by which a demand is presented for the mention
of a subject and an object: so it happen that for the designation
of the subject you employ the word *object,* then so it will be
that for the designation of that which may, with propriety, be

termed the subject, finding the only proper word preoccupied, you will naturally feel yourself at a loss.

In a case where the faculty of the will is not considered as having any part, the designation of *the end in view* is a function in which any occasion for the employment of the word object, cannot have place; in this case, therefore, neither has the uncertainty which, as above, is liable to be produced by that word.

In a case where the will is supposed to be employed, and in which there is, accordingly, an *end in view,* one single end to the attainment of which by the power and under the orders of the will the action is directed, in any such case what may very well happen is, that there shall be other entities to which, in the course of the action, though not in the characters of *ends in view,* it may happen to the attention to be directed. Here, then, besides an object which may be, will be other objects, no one of which can commodiously be designated by the compound appellation, *end in view.*

In regard to the word *subject,* (as well as the word object,) one convenience is, that it may be used in the plural number. This convenience belongs to them in contradistinction to the word field. For a group of numerous and comparatively small entities, the word field will not, either in the singular or in the plural, conveniently serve; but to this same purpose the word subject, if employed in the plural, is perfectly well adapted.

If, beneath the imagined line of action, you have need to bring to view not merely one extensive fictitious immoveable body, but a multitude of smaller moveable bodies lying on it, here comes an occasion for the use of both these terms: viz. field and subject, or subjects; the field is the extensive immoveable entity, the subjects the comparatively numerous and less extensive bodies, fixed or lying loose upon the surface of it.

In the place of the word *field,* as well as in place of the word *subject,* the words *subject-matter* may be employed; so also the plural, subject-matters. But if, in addition to an extensive surface, you have to bring to view a multitude of smaller bodies stationed on it; if, in that case, instead of the word *field,* you employ the words *subject-matters,* you will find that you cannot commodiously, after laying down your subject-matter, have subjects stationed on it.

In the case where the action in question is a physical, a corporeal one, a question might perhaps arise whether the entities respectively designated by the words subject and object, belong to the class of real or fictitious entities: a platform on which you stand to shoot an arrow, a butt at which you shoot your arrow, to these could not be refused the appellation of real entities. But in so far as upon the platform you superinduce the character designated by the word subject, and upon the *butt* the character designated by the word object; of this subject and this object it might be insisted that they are but so many names of fictitious entities.

Not that for any practical purpose, a question thus turning upon mere words would be, in any considerable degree, worthy of regard.

Be this as it may, in the case in which the action in question is an incorporeal, a psychical action, having no other field than the mind, or than what is in the mind, – in this case the title of the words subject and object, as well as of the word field, to the appellation of fictitious entities, will be seen to be clear of doubt.

SECTION VII.
Concomitant Fictitious Entities resulting from the process of Logical aggregation and division, and subalternation.

It will be seen further on more at large, how it is, that when contemplating the qualities exhibited by individuals, by abstracting the attention successively from them, quality after quality, let the group of individuals, present, past and future, contingent included, be ever so vast and multitudinous, there will, at last, be left some quality, or assemblage of qualities, which, being found all of them existing in a certain assemblage of individuals, and not in any other, may serve for the foundation of a name by which that whole assemblage may be designated, without including in the designation any individual not included in that assemblage. The words, mineral, vegetable, animal, may serve for examples.

Wherever any such aggregate number of individuals can

be found so connected with one another, – so distinguished from all others, and, for the designation of the aggregate, the *fictitious unit* composed of that multitude, a name or appellation has been employed, and appropriated by use, the fictitious unit thus formed will be found capable of being divided by the imagination into lesser component aggregates or units, – these again each of them into others; and, in this way, the largest and first divided all-comprehensive aggregate will be found capable of being divided and sub-divided into any number of aggregates, not greater than the whole number of individuals, actual and conceivable, contained in the original factitious and fictitious whole, – the name of each one of these component aggregates constituting, as it were, a box for containing and keeping together the several aggregates comprised in it, the entire aggregate contained in each such box being characterized by some quality or qualities in respect of which being agreed with one another, at the same time they disagree with, and are thereby distinguished from all others.

Kingdom, class, order, genus, species, variety, have been the names given to these boxes – to these factitious receptacles.

That it is to the class of fictitious, and not to the class of real entities, that these imaginary, however really useful receptacles, appertain, is, at this time of day, sufficiently clear; but the time has been when they have been mistaken for realities.

SECTION VIII.
Political and Quasi *Political Fictitious Entities.*

I. EFFECTS. – 1. Obligation; 2. Right; 4. Exemption; 4. Power; 5. Privilege; 6. Prerogative; 7. Possession – physical; 8. Possession – legal; 9. Property.

II. CAUSES. – 1. Command; 2. Prohibition, Inhibition, &c.; 3. Punishment; 4. Pardon; 5. License; 6. Warrant; 7. Judgment; 8. Division.

All these have for their efficient causes pleasure and pain, but principally pain, in whatsoever shape, and from which soever of the five sanctions or sources of pleasure or pain, derived or expected, viz. – 1. The physical sanction; 2. The sympathetic sanction, or sanction of sympathy; 3. The popular or moral sanction; 4. The political, including the legal sanction; 5. The religious sanction.

Obligation is the root out of which all these other fictitious entities take their rise.

Of all the sanctions or sources of pleasure and pain above brought to view, the political sanction being susceptible of being the strongest and surest in its operation, and, accordingly, the obligation derived from it the strongest and most effective, this is the sanction which it seems advisable to take for consideration in the first instance; the correspondent obligations of the same name which may be considered as emanating from these other fictitious entities being, in the instance of some of these sanctions, of too weak a nature to act with any sufficient force capable of giving to any of those other productions any practical value.

An obligation, – understand here that sort of obligation which, through the medium of the will, operates on the active faculty, – takes its nature from some act to which it applies itself; it is an obligation to perform or to abstain from performing a certain act.

A legal obligation to perform the act in question is said to attach upon a man, to be incumbent upon him, in so far as in the event of his performing the act, (understand both at the time and place in question,) he will not suffer any pain, but in the event of his not performing it he will suffer a certain pain, viz. the pain that corresponds to it, and by the virtue of which applying itself eventually as above, the obligation is created.

SECTION IX.
Fictitious Entities appertaining to Relation as between Cause and Effect.

In the idea of causation, – in the idea of the relation as between cause and effect, – in the idea of the operation or state of things by which that relation is produced, in which that relation takes its rise, the idea of motion is inseparably involved: take away motion, no causation can have place, – no result, no effect, no *any*-thing can be produced.

In the idea of *motion,* the idea of *a moving body* is, with equal necessity, implied.

Of the cases in which the existence of motion, relative motion, is reported to us by our senses, there are some in which the commencement of the motion is, others in which it is not manifest to our senses.

Endless and terminating. Under one or other of these denominations may all motions, observed or observable, be included.

Endless motions are those which have place among the bodies, (each of them considered in its totality,) of which the visible universe is composed.

To the class of terminating or terminative motions belong all those which have place in our planet, and, to judge from analogy, all those which have place in any other of the celestial bodies.

So far as the motions in question belong to the endless class, so far no such distinction, and, therefore, no such relation as that of cause and effect, seems to have place. Each body attracts towards it all the rest, and, were it to have place singly, the attraction thus exercised might be considered as if it operated in the character of a *cause;* but each body is attracted by every other, and, were it to have place singly, the attraction thus suffered might be considered in the character of an *effect*. But, in fact, the two words are but two different names for one and the same effect. In the case of motions that have place among the distinct bodies with which the surface of our earth is covered, action and causation are the phenomena exhibited by different bodies in the character of agents and patients. In the case of the celestial bodies, considered each in its totality, no such distinction has place. No such character as that of agent – no such character as that of patient, belongs separately to any one. They are each one of them agent and patient at the same time. No one exhibits more of agency, no one more of patiency, than any other.

Suppose that all these several bodies having been created out of nothing at one and the same instant, each with the same quantity of matter, and thence with the same attractive power that appears to belong to it at present, an impulse in a certain rectilinear direction were to be given to each of them at the same time. On this hypothesis it has been rendered, it is said, matter of demonstration, that the sort of intermediate motions which would be the result, would be exactly those which these same bodies are found by observation to exhibit.

Here, then, we should have a beginning, but even here we should not have an end. In the beginning, at a determinate point of time, we should have a motion operating in the character of a cause, but at no determinate point of time, to the exclusion of any other, should we have either a motion or a new order of things resulting from it, and produced by it, in the character of an effect.

Thelematic and *athelematic*. – To one or other of these denominations will all motions of the terminative class be found referable. *Thelematic,* those in the production of which *volition,* the mind of a sentient and self-moving being, is seen to be concerned. *Athelematic,* those in the production of which volition is not seen to have place.

In the case of a motion of the thelematic class, you have for the *cause* of the motion, – meaning the *prime* cause of whatsoever motion happens in consequence to take place, the physical act, the act of the will of the person by whose will the motion is produced; you have that same person for the agent.

Fruitful or unfruitful, or, say *ergastic* or *unergastic*. – To one or other of these denominations will all the motions of the thelematic class be found referable. *Ergastic* or fruitful, all those which have for their termination and result the production of *a work*. *Unergastic* or unfruitful, all those which are not attended with any such result.

Between these two classes the line of separation, it will be manifest enough, cannot, in the nature of the case, be determinate.

A work has reference to human interests and exigencies. When, in consequence of a motion, or set of motions, of the thelematic kind, in the body or among the bodies in which the motion has terminated, or those to which it has in the whole, or in any part, been communicated, any such change of condition has place, by which, for any considerable portion of time, they are or are not regarded as being rendered, in any fresh shape, subservient to human use, *a work* is spoken of as having thereby been produced.

In so far as a work is considered as having been produced, any agent, who, in respect of his active talent, is regarded as having borne the principal part in the production of the work, is wont to be spoken of under the appellation of *an author* or *the author*.

In this same case any body which is regarded as having, in consequence of the motion communicated to it, been rendered contributory to the production of the work, is wont to be spoken of in the character, and by the name, of an instrument, – any *body,* viz. inasmuch as considered as inanimate – *an instrument* in the *physical* sense; if animated, or considered as animated, and, in particular, if regarded as *rational* – in the *physical* sense; if regarded as *simple,* a tool or implement; if regarded as *complex,* an engine, a machine, – a system of machinery.

To the case, and to that alone, in which the motion or motions, being of the *thelematic,* and therein, moreover, of the *ergastic* kind, have had for their prime mover or principal agent concerned, a rational, or at least, a sentient, being, belong the words *end, operation, means, design.*

Of the word *end,* and its synonym, the compound term, *end in view,* the exposition has been already given. It consists in the idea of some good (*i.e.* pleasure, or exemption from pain in this or that shape or shapes) as about eventually to result to the agent in question from the proposed act in question.

Operation is a name given to any action in so far as it is considered as having been performed in the endeavour to produce a work.

The word *means* is a term alike applicable, with propriety, to the designation of body considered in the character of an *instrument,* or any *action* or *motion* considered in the character of an *operation,* tending to the production of *a work,* or any good looked to in the character of *an end.*

Productive and *unproductive,* – under one or other of these denominations, as the case may be, may be referred the action in question, in so far as where, being of the *thelematic,* and, moreover, of the *ergastic kind,* it has for its *end in view* the bringing into existence any intended result in the character of *a work.*

Productive and *unproductive,* whether in actual result or only in tendency, under one or other of these denominations may also be referred every motion, or set of motions, of the *athelematic kind*; every motion, or set of motions, produced in, by and upon such agents as are of the purely physical kind.

This distinction is applicable to all the three physical kingdoms; but, on the mention of it, the two living kingdoms, the vegetable and the animal, will be most apt to present themselves.

In the use frequently made of the word *cause,* may be seen an ambiguity, which, in respect of its incompatibility with any correct and clear view of the relation between cause and effect, there may be a practical use in endeavouring to remove from the field of thought and language.

On the one hand, *a motion, an action, an operation;* on the other hand, *an agent, an operator, an author*; to the designation of both these, in themselves perfectly distinct objects, the words are wont to be indiscriminately applied.

Take, for example, the questions that used to be agitated in the logical schools. Is the moon, says one of them, the cause, or a cause, of the flux and reflux of the sea? Here the moon, here the word cause is employed to designate a corporeal being considered in the character of an agent.

The cause, (says a position of which frequent use was made in the same theatres of disputation,) *the cause is always proportioned to its effect.* But, between the moon itself and the tide, *i.e.* the flux and reflux of the sea, there cannot be any proportion; they are *disparate* entities, the one *the moon,* a real entity, the other, the flux and reflux, *i.e.* the motions of the sea are but fictitious entities. Between the moon itself, and the water moved by it, *i.e.* between the quantity of both, proportion may have place; between the motion, and thence the action of the moon, and the motion of the waters, a proportion may have place. But, between the moon, a body, and the flux and reflux of the sea, no proportion can have place, neither can either be larger or smaller than the other.

In speaking of God, it has been common to speak of that inferential. Being by such names as *the Cause of all things, the great, the universal Cause.* In this instance, the same sort of confusion, the same sort of indistinctness in the expression, the same consequent confusion in men's conception, as in the case mentioned, is apt to have place.

The *act* of God, the *will* of God, – these are the entities, to the designation of which, and which alone, the term *cause* can, in the case in question, with propriety, and consistently with analogy, be employed; these, on the one hand, and the word *cause* on the other, are alike names of fictitious entities.

Author, and Creator, – these alone, and not the word cause, can, with propriety, be employed in speaking of God. These, as well as God, are names of real entities; not names of fictitious entities: Author, a name applicable to man, or, in a word, to any being considered as susceptible of design; Creator, a term exclusively appropriated to the designation of *God,* considered with reference to his works.

In the use commonly made of the terms, *work, cause, effect, instrument,* and in the habit of prefixing to them respectively the definitive article *the,* seems to be implied a notion, of which the more closely it is examined, the more plainly will the incorrectness be made to appear, – this is, that where the effect is considered as one, there exists some one object, and no more than one, which, with propriety, can be considered as its cause. Of the exemplification and verification of this supposition, there exists not, perhaps, so much as a single instance.

Take, in the first place, an effect, any effect, of the physical kind; – no effect of this kind can, it is believed, be assigned, that is not the result of a multitude of influencing circumstances; some always, in different ways, contributing to the production of it, viz. in the character of promoting and co-operating *causes*; others frequently contributing to the non-production of it, in the character of obstacles.

In relation to the result in question, considered in the character of an *effect,* suppose, at pleasure, any one body to be the *prime or principal* mover or agent, and the motion, the action, or the operation of it, to be the *prime* or principal *cause.*

In no instance can any such cause be in operation, but it will happen to it to be, on all sides, encompassed and surrounded by *circumstances*.

Those circumstances will consist of the state of the contiguous and surrounding bodies, in respect of motion or rest, form, colour, quantity, and the like.

Among these some will appear to be exercising on the result a material operative influence; others not to be exercising such influence. Influential and influencing circumstances, uninfluential or uninfluencing circumstances; in one or other of these two classes of circumstances taken together, will every circumstance by which it can happen to the principal agent or agents to be encompassed, be comprised.

Promotive or *obstructive,* – under one or other of these denominations may the whole assemblage of influential circumstances be comprised.

Any circumstances that act, that are considered as acting in the character of *obstructive* circumstances, are termed, in one word, *Obstacles.*

Purely natural, purely factitious, and mixed, – to one or other of these heads may every motion be referred, considered with reference to the part which the human will is capable of bearing in the production of it.

Solid, liquid, or gaseous, – in one or other of these states, at the time of the motion, will the moving body be found.

The internal constitution of the moving body, the internal constitution of the unmoveable, or non-moving bodies, with which it comes in contact, and the configuration of these same bodies; – upon all these several circumstances, or rather groups of circumstances, must the nature of the ultimate effect produced by the motion be dependent, – whether that effect be a purely physical result, or a human work.

In so far then as, by the term *cause,* nothing more is meant to be designated than one alone of all those sets of co-operating circumstances; be the effect what it may, the cause can never of itself be adequate to the production of it; nor, between the quantum of the effect and the quantum of the cause, can any determinate proportion have place.

But, of the case in which, in the extent given to the import attributed to the word *cause,* the whole assemblage of these influencing circumstances is taken into the account and comprised, it seems questionable whether so much as a single example would be to be found.

Unless the above observations be altogether incorrect, it will appear but too manifest that, in the notions commonly attached to the word *cause,* much deficiency, in respect of clearness and correctness, as well as completeness, cannot but have place; and that, in the inferences made from either e one to the other, whether it be the cause that is deduced, or supposed to be deduced, from the effect, or the effect that is deduced, or supposed to be deduced, from the cause, much uncertainty and inconclusiveness cannot but be a frequent, not to say an almost constant and continual, result.

Seldom, indeed, does it happen that, of the co-influencing circumstances, the collection made for the purpose is complete; nor is it always that, in such a collection, so much as the principally influencing circumstances are included.

In those cases in which the several influencing circumstances are, all of them, subject, not only to the observation, but to the powers of human agency, any such miscalculations and errors as from time to time happen to be made, may, when perceived from time to time, be corrected.

Thus it is, for example, in the case of observations that have for their field the anatomy and physiology of plants and animals.

Thus it is, moreover, with little exception in the instance of the practical applications made of the respective theories of Chemistry and Mechanics, the influencing circumstances being, for the most part, or even altogether subject, and that, at all times, not only to our observations, but to our command.

The cases in which our inferences from supposed causes to supposed effects, and from supposed effects to supposed causes, seem most precarious and exposed to error, are, – on the one hand, cases belonging to the field of medicine, on the other hand, cases belonging to the field of naval architecture.

In cases belonging to the field of *medicine,* the influencing circumstances belonging principally to the class of chemical phenomena – to those phenomena by which particular sorts of bodies are distinguished from each other, lie, in a great degree, out of the reach of our observation.

In cases belonging to the field of naval architecture, the influencing circumstances, belonging principally to the class of mechanical phenomena, – to those phenomena which belong in common to bodies in general, may, perhaps, in *specie* be, without much difficulty, comprehended in their totality by observation; but, in respect of their *quantity,* lie, in a great measure, beyond even the reach of *observation,* and, in a still greater degree, are out of the reach of *command.*

Prone as is the human mind to the making of hasty

and imperfectly-grounded inductions on the field of physical science, it cannot but be much more so in the fields of psychology and ethics, in which is included the field of politics; commonly not only is the collection made of *influencing* circumstances incomplete, but *uninfluencing* circumstances, and even *obstacles,* are placed in the station of, and held up to view in the character of, principally or even exclusively operating causes.

Thus superior is the density of the clouds which overhang the relation between cause and effect in the field of morals, as compared with the field of physics. Two concurring considerations may help us to account for this difference, – 1. The elements of calculation being in so large a proportion of the psychical class – such as intentions, affections, and motives, – are, in a proportional degree, situated out of the reach of direct observation. 2. In the making of the calculation, the judgment is, in a peculiar degree, liable to be disturbed and led astray by the several sources of illusion, – by original intellectual weakness, by sinister interest, by interest-begotten prejudice, and by adopted prejudice.

Material, formal, efficient, final, – by these terms in the language of the Aristotelian schools – by these terms, in the higher forms of common language, so many different species of causes are considered as designated.

Neither incapable of being applied to practice, nor of being ever applied with advantage, these distinctions present, in this place, a just claim to notice. The relation they bear to the foregoing exposition, will now be brought to view.

Matter and *form,* – both these, it has been seen, are necessary to existence, – meaning, to real and that physical existence, – the existence of a physical body.

1. By *material cause* is indicated the matter of the body in question, considered in so far as it is regarded as contributing to the production of the effect in question.

2. By *formal cause,* the form of the same body.

3. By *efficient cause* must be understood, in so far as any clear and distinct idea is attached to the term, the matter of some body or bodies: what is meant to be distinguished by may, in general, be supposed to be the motion of that body, ssemblage of bodies, which is regarded as the principal

motion, – the motion which has the principal share in the production of the effect.

But to the production of the effect, – meaning a physical effect, – whatsoever it be, a correspondent and suitable disposition of the circumjacent non-moving bodies is not (it has been seen) less necessary than a correspondent and suitable motion, or aggregate of motions, on the part of the moving body.

To the designation of the *matter,* and of the *form,* that concurs in the production of the effect, the language here in question is, therefore, we see, adequate; but, to the designation of the other influencing circumstances, we see how far it is from being adequate.

4. By final cause, is meant the *end* which the agent had in view; meaning, as hath been seen, by the *end,* if anything at all be meant by it, the good to the attainment of which the act was directed, – the good, *i.e.* the pleasure, or pleasures, the exemption or security from such or such pain, or pains.

It is, therefore, only in so far as the effect is the result of design on the part of a sensitive being; a being susceptible of pains and pleasures, – of those sensations which, by us, are experienced and known by the names of pleasures and pains, that the species of cause here called *final* can have place.

The doctrine of final causes supposes, therefore, on the part of the agent in question, the experience of pleasure and pain; of pleasures and pains, the same as those of which we have experience – for to us there are no others; employed in any such attempt as that of designating and bringing to view the idea of any others, they would be employed in designating and bringing to view so many non-entities.

SECTION X.
Existence, and the Classes of Fictitious Entities related to it.

Existence is a quality, the most extensively applicable, and, at the same time, the most simple of all qualities actual or imaginable. Take away all other qualities, this remains: to speak more strictly, take any entity whatsoever, real or fictitious, – abstract the attention from whatsoever other qualities may have been found belonging to it, this will still be left. *Existence* is predicable of naked *substance*.

Opposite to the idea of existence is that of non-existence. Non-existence is the negation of existence. Of every other entity, real or fictitious, either *existence* or *non-existence* is at all times predicable. Whether such other entity be real or fictitious, its existence is, of course, a fictitious entity; *i.e.* the word existence is, in all cases, the name of a fictitious entity.

The idea of *non-existence* is the idea of *absence* extended. Take any *place*, and therewith, any real entity – any body existing in that place, suppose it no longer existing in that place, you suppose its *absence*, its *relative* non-existence. Expel it, in like manner, from every, from all, place, you suppose its *absolute* non-existence.

It is through the medium of absence, the familiar and continually recurring idea of absence, that the idea of non-existence, the terrific, the transcendant, the awful, and imposing idea of non-existence is attained.

Existence being, as above, a species of quality, is itself a fictitious entity; – it is in every real entity – every real entity is in it.

In it, the man, the object of whose appetite is the sublime, and he the object of whose appetite is the ridiculous, may here find matter for their respective banquets. *Nothing* has been laughed at to satiety. The punster who has played with *nothing* till he is tired may renew the game with existence and non-existence.

At any point of time, in any place whatsoever, take any entity, any real entity whatsoever, between its existence in that place and its non-existence in that same place, there is not any *alternative*, there is not any *medium* whatsoever.

Necessity, impossibility, certainty, uncertainty, probability, improbability, actuality, potentiality; – whatsoever there is of reality correspondent to any of these names, is nothing more or less than a disposition, a persuasion of the mind, on the part of him by whom these words are employed, in relation to the state of things, or the event or events to which these qualities are ascribed.

Down to the present time, whatsoever be this present time, whether the time of writing this, or the time of any one's reading it, whatsoever has existed has had existence, – whatsoever has not existed has not had existence; at this time whatsoever does exist, has existence, – whatsoever does not exist has not existence; and so at any and every future point of time. Throughout the whole expanse of time, past, present, and future, put together, where will room be found for anything real to answer to any of these names?

Quality itself is but a fictitious entity, but these are all of them so many fictitious qualities. They do not, as real qualities, – they do not, like gravity, solidity, roundness, hardness, belong to the objects themselves to which they are ascribed, – in the character of attributes of the objects to which they are ascribed, they are mere chimeras, mere creatures of the imagination – nonentities.

Yet, nonentities as they are, but too real is the mischief of which some of them, and, in particular, the word *necessity,* has been productive: – antipathy, strife, persecution, murder upon a national, upon an international, scale.

The persuasion expressed by the word *certainty* has for its foundation the event itself simply. The persuasion indicated by the word *necessity* has for its object not only that event, but an infinity of other events, and states of things out of number, from the beginning of time, in the character of its *causes.*

Certainty, necessity, impossibility; exhibited seriously in any other character than that of expressions of the degree of the persuasion entertained in relation to the subject in question, by him whose words they are, in the use of these words is virtually involved the assumption of omniscience. All things that are possible are within my knowledge, – this is not upon the list; such being interpreted is the phrase, *this thing is impossible.*

The sort of occasion on which, without any such assumption, these terms can be applied, is that of a contradiction in terms, – a self-contradictory proposition, or two mutually contradictory propositions issuing, at the same time, from the same mouth or the same pen. But here the objects to which these attributes are, with propriety, applicable, are not the objects, for the designation of which the propositions are applied, but the propositions themselves. Propositions thus contradictory and incompatible cannot, with propriety, be applied to the same object. It is impossible that they should, *i.e.* inconsistent with the notions entertained by the person in question, in relation to what is proper and what improper in language.

It is impossible that, among a multitude of bodies all equal to one another, four taken together should not be greater than two taken together. Why? Because, by the word *four* has, by every person, been designated a number greater than by the word *two*.

Yet, in affirmance of the truth of a proposition thus impossible, persuasion rising to the highest pitch of intensity has been entertained. Why? Because the human mind having it in its power to apply itself to any object, or to forbear to apply to itself at pleasure, the person in question has exercised this power in relation to the import of the words in question, as above, *i.e.* to the import which, according to his experience, all persons by whom they have been employed have been constantly in the habit of annexing to them. But against an object which the mind has contrived to exclude out of the field of its attention, no objection can, in that same field, be seen to bear. Whatsoever, therefore, were the considerations by which he was engaged to endeavour to persuade himself of the truth of the self-contradictory, and therefore, impossible, propositions, remain without anything to counteract their force.

Radial Thinkers